FAITH
and
FURY

The Temple Mount and the Noble Sanctuary: The Story of Jerusalem's Most Sacred Space

Ilene Cooper

Roaring Brook Press
New York

Photo Credits

A. Abbas/Magnum Photos: p. 116; AFP/Handout/Getty Images: p. 106; Archives/REX/Shutterstock: p. 28 (upper); Bettmann/Getty Images: p. 101; BibleLandPictures.com/Alamy Stock Photo: p. 67; Courtesy of the Visual Instruction Department Lantern Slides Collection, Special Collections and Archives Research Center, Oregon State University Libraries: p. 89; David Rubinger/Contributor/ Getty Images: p. 111; dbimages/Alamy Stock Photo: p. 62; Fondation Gilles-Caron/Contributor/Getty Images: p. 109; HolyLandPhotos.org: pp. 8, 39, 44, 45; John Phillips/Contributor/Getty Images: p. 105; Leo Kann/Stringer/Getty Images: p. 102; Library of Congress, Prints & Photographs Division: p. 79; Micha Bar Am/Magnum Photos: p. 113; Michele Falzone/Alamy Stock Photo: p. 23; New York Public Library: pp. 94, 96, 98; Ritmeyer Archaeological Design: pp. 16, 19, 49; Sonia Halliday Photo Library/Alamy Stock Photo: p. 85; Z. Radovan/BibleLandPictures: pp. xii, 9, 12, 27, 28 (lower), 30, 31, 41, 43, 58, 59, 60, 66, 80, 87, 88, 90.

Library of Congress Cataloging-in-Publication Data

Names: Cooper, Ilene, author.
Title: Faith and Fury : the Temple Mount and the Noble Sanctuary: the story of Jerusalem's most
    sacred space / Ilene Cooper.
Description: First edition. | New York : Roaring Brook Press, 2017.
Identifiers: LCCN 2015034422 | ISBN 9781596435308 (hardback)
Subjects: LCSH: Temple Mount (Jerusalem)—Juvenile literature. | BISAC: JUVENILE
NONFICTION / History / Middle East. | JUVENILE NONFICTION / Religion / General.
Classification: LCC DS109.28 .C66 2016 | DDC 956.94/42—dc23
LC record available at https://lccn.loc.gov/2015034422

Our books may be purchased in bulk for promotional, educational, or business use. Please
contact your local bookseller or the Macmillan Corporate and Premium Sales Department
at (800) 221-7945 ext. 5442 or by e-mail at MacmillanSpecialMarkets@macmillan.com.

First edition, 2017
Book design by Roberta Pressel
Illustrations by Thomas LaPadula
Maps designed by Cathy Bobak
Printed in the United States of America by LSC Communications, Harrisonburg, Virginia

10 9 8 7 6 5 4 3 2 1

For those of every faith who pray and hope for peace
And for my brother

CONTENTS

AUTHOR'S NOTE

When I conceived the idea for a book about what is commonly referred to in the West as Jerusalem's Temple Mount, the premise was simple: to introduce readers to a place that is holy to three religions—Judaism, Christianity, and Islam—yet over the millennia has almost continually been wrapped in fighting, bloodshed, and tears. My questions were: Why hasn't a place that is so revered brought out the best in people instead of the worst? And: What might it mean for the world if peace could come to this very small piece of real estate? I quickly learned that while the idea for the book might be simple, writing it was going to be difficult.

The problems were multiple in nature. First, there was the matter of explaining the history. Almost everything we know about early Jewish history and Solomon's Temple comes from the Bible. Naturally, readers—especially young readers—want to know what is "true" and what is "not true." I have tried to show when archaeological evidence supports a particular account, while noting that some people consider biblical stories to be factual. Still other people, though they may not believe the incidents recounted in the Bible to be fact per se, understand that the stories' narrative power has given them a weight over the centuries. I have used the time designations BCE, "before the Common Era," and CE, "Common Era," for the early historical periods, and the accompanying time line should help readers visualize when these events were occurring (or are said to have occurred) in history.

As for nomenclature, in Jewish, Christian, and wider-ranging contexts I have used the term "Temple Mount," because that is what most Western books on the subject use, but in Muslim contexts I have used the term "Noble Sanctuary." I also use the term "Hebrew Bible" to refer to what is sometimes called the Old Testament, a designation that is not compatible with how Jews view their sacred text. The term "Torah" refers to the first five books of the Hebrew Bible: Genesis, Exodus, Leviticus, Numbers, and Deuteronomy.

Spellings were problematic throughout. For instance, the name of the Muslim sultan is regularly seen as Suleiman, Suleyman, and Süleyman. I have used the spellings I have found to be most common and easiest for a young audience. Dates, especially in the BCE period, varied. I have marked dates as "approximately" to note this.

Another hurdle was giving equal weight to the perceptions and tenets of three religions, all claiming to descend from Abraham, but which have more often seen one another as rivals than as relatives. I have tried to accomplish this by following the history, however tangled it becomes, using several sources as arbitrators when the material became difficult to reconcile. The two authors I turned to most often were Karen Armstrong, the award-winning British writer known for her books on comparative religion, and Hershel Shanks, the founder of the Biblical Archaeology Society, and the editor of the *Biblical Archaeology Review*. He has also written numerous books and articles on biblical history. Any mistakes, however, are of course my own.

When quoting from the Bible, I have used several translations, choosing the version that I felt was most suitable or understandable for a young audience, and these are identified in the source notes. Sometimes the devil was in the details. For instance, take a simple question: How big is (or was) the Temple Mount? For some reason, the usual comparison is to football fields. But how many? I read twenty-five football fields, thirty, twenty-one. Finally, I decided to write "more than twenty." Then someone asked if the writers meant American football fields! So questions of how, when, and where were sometimes up for debate. Certainly questions of why depended on who was telling a particular story, and I have tried to make clear from whose perspective various incidents are being reported.

When it came to the more recent struggle between the Palestinians and the Israelis, my goal was to simply report the facts, acknowledging but not emphasizing the anguish on both sides caused by the ongoing struggle. How these struggles may play out in coming years as they concern the Temple Mount is more speculative, but there has certainly been—and continues to be—enough strife around the site to make educated guesses. When there are troubles, it is always the hope that cooler heads will prevail, but with so many competing intra- as well as interreligious struggles, it gets more difficult to see that happening. Still, I wanted to end the book on an optimistic note, which took me back to one of my bedrock beliefs, the power of the Golden Rule. Karen Armstrong has started an organization called Charter for Compassion (charterforcompassion.org), whose goal is to make the world a more understanding place. From their mission statement: "We believe that a compassionate world is possible when every man, woman and child treats others as they wish to be treated—with dignity, equity and respect. We believe that all human beings are born with the capacity for compassion, and that it must be cultivated for human beings to survive and thrive."

The road to compassion in the Middle East has been arduous. But where there is life, there is hope.

Jerusalem: stone walls surround the Temple Mount and the Old City.

PROLOGUE

In the city of Jerusalem stands a place that is covered in prayer, soaked with tears, and awash with blood. For thousands of years, hope and fear, hatred and love have mingled there, all in the name of God. Jews and Christians call this holy site the Temple Mount. To Muslims, it is Haram al-Sharif, the Noble Sanctuary.

The name Temple Mount comes from the Jewish temples that once stood on this elevated area. In the seventh century it became home to Muslim religious buildings. At the very end of the eleventh century, Christian Crusaders captured the Mount and turned those buildings into churches. Since 1187, when Jerusalem was retaken, this place of spiritual history has once again been in Muslim hands. Myths and stories have risen around this spot, which in ancient times was only a bare, rocky plateau rising more than 2,000 feet above sea level. Some say God found the dust to form Adam there. Others claim it was the location of the Garden of Eden. Familiar religious names have all been linked to this space: Abraham, David, Solomon, Jesus, Muhammad.

Today, as in the past, the Temple Mount/the Noble Sanctuary dominates the Jerusalem skyline, rising up from the Old City. The Old City is a small part of modern Jerusalem, surrounded by stone walls built in the sixteenth century by the Turkish ruler Suleiman the Magnificent. It is loosely divided into four sections: Christian to the northwest; Muslim to the northeast; Jewish to the southeast; and Armenian to the southwest.

There are seven gates to enter the Old City, but the most heavily used is the Jaffa Gate, on the western side of town. Once inside, it feels like you are stepping back in time. Move through the narrow cobblestoned streets, past the covered markets, and it's hard to know which century you are in until a spark of modernity pushes you off balance. Here the old and new mingle and sometimes clash. People balancing large tray-like baskets on their heads bearing bread or fruit walk by visitors chattering on cell phones. Men and women in religious dress pass others wearing jeans and T-shirts. This mix of colors, sights, and sounds takes place in the shadow of important historical events, both ancient and modern.

Walk through the souk, the lively Arab marketplace, and continue into the Jewish Quarter. Pass the Cardo, a market spot since Roman times that is now home to fancy shops, and stroll along the winding streets until you see signs that, in English, say THE TEMPLE MOUNT. Come to a security checkpoint, and you have arrived. You are about to enter one of the holiest spots on earth.

Ahead is an open-air prayer plaza and a stretch of stone wall almost two hundred feet long and more than 2,000 years old. The wall was once thought to be part of the huge Jewish temple built by Herod the Great and destroyed by the Romans in 70 CE. In fact, the Western Wall is only a retaining wall that helped support the huge platform on which the temple once stood. Still, this remnant is the holiest site in Jewish tradition. People flock there to pray, contemplate, and place within its cracks prayers of hope and messages of gratitude. For Jewish believers, God's divine presence still hovers over the Western Wall.

Above the Western Wall is the large expanse covering the same area that once held the Jewish temple. Today, it is home to some of the most important buildings in the Muslim world, including the Al-Aqsa Mosque, at the southern end of what the Islamic world calls the Noble Sanctuary. However, it is the Dome of the Rock, a building of outstanding beauty, that is the focal point. The building's exterior is covered with glazed tiles dominated by those colored a heavenly blue. It is topped with a golden dome that shines brilliantly against the Jerusalem sky.

This structure is a Muslim shrine built to house a rock. Jews and Christians revere this rock as well. Step inside the magnificent edifice constructed with marble pillars covered with intricate mosaics, and it is startling to realize all this beauty is in service to a rough-hewn piece of stone. Lying directly under the golden dome, it juts up above floor level. Gray and massive, it is pockmarked with slashes, some natural, some man-made. If this rock were not encased in such splendor, perhaps it would seem like any other. But it is like no other. And it is at this rock that the story starts.

1

BEFORE THE TEMPLE

Four thousand years ago the stony outcrop near the top of a mountain may have already been a holy place for the Canaanites, a people often mentioned in the Bible, some of whom lived in an area west of the River Jordan that would eventually become ancient Israel.

There are places on earth that are thought of as sacred spaces, and this mountaintop was a sacred space in ancient times. What is a sacred space? Just as today you might feel closer to God or a higher power in a building of worship or camping out in a forest of tall trees, from the beginning of civilization, people have experienced those same strong emotions. There were places—some majestic like mountains, some more intimate like a hidden bubbling spring—where men, women, and children felt as if they were close to something larger than themselves and outside their everyday experiences.

Altars or temples were often built to mark these spots. And when a community was invaded by a new tribe or civilization, its holy sites were often appropriated by the newcomers. Archaeologists believe this particular rocky place was sacred to those who worshipped the

Canaanite god Baal. But the first time it is written about is in the biblical story of Abraham and Isaac.

Abraham is revered among Jews, Christians, and Muslims. We meet him in Genesis, the first book of the Bible. In the ancient world people usually prayed to many gods, but Abraham, tradition tells us, believed that there was only one God. God found Abraham and they made a promise to each other—also known as a covenant. Abraham would accept the Lord as his God and, in return, the Lord would provide him with his own land—the land of Canaan—and make him the father of many nations. But as the story is told in the Book of Genesis, the Lord later made a startling request of Abraham. He was to take his son Isaac, and find a particular mountain of God's choosing, in an area called Moriah. There, Abraham was to slay Isaac and then make him a burnt offering to the Lord. Without question, Abraham took Isaac to the mountain, tied him to a pyre of wood, and was about to kill him with his knife when an angel appeared and stayed his hand. God was now assured of Abraham's submission to His will. Abraham then spied a ram in a nearby thicket and captured it to use as an offering in place of his son.

This unsettling, even horrific story and its meaning have been discussed and debated for thousands of years. Jews and Christians call the tale "The Binding of Isaac." Muslims, who revere another of Abraham's sons, Ishmael, as the father of the Arab people, believe that Ishmael was the son to be sacrificed. Few who hear this story ever forget it, and because the story is remembered, so is the place where it happened, which traditions tell us is the rocky outcrop that would later become the site of the Temple Mount.

Is any of this true? Other than in religious books like the Bible and the Quran, there is no mention in recorded history of the man named Abraham. Archaeology is silent on whether any or none of this happened. But millions around the world have believed and continue to believe that the accounts in the Bible are of actual events. Others may not take the stories as fact, but still find them to have power and meaning.

Religious scholars place the time of the writing of Abraham's story about 1,800 years before the birth of Jesus, almost 4,000 years ago. Other stories in the Book of Genesis continue the family tales. Isaac had his own sons, one of whom was Jacob. During an arduous journey, Jacob laid his head down on a rock and dreamed of wrestling with an angel, which convinced him he was in a sacred place. Though the name of the location is not mentioned, that holy place, where an angel appeared, also became associated through legend with the rocky top of Mount Moriah.

Bible stories and archaeology began to merge when a town grew up around the mountain range of which Moriah was a part— Jerusalem. Bits of pottery and tombs dating back 5,000 years have been found in the area south of the oldest parts of today's Jerusalem. It was then just a settlement, though archaeology shows that there were actual towns in Canaan. One still in existence today is Jericho. But those towns were closer either to the coast of the Mediterranean Sea or to desert trade routes. The area that would become Jerusalem sat at the crest of the low range of mountains located between the fertile coastal area and the hot Judaean desert. It was not a particularly easy place to defend, a disadvantage at a time when local tribes were constantly fighting with one another.

But one thing this settlement did have was water, the Gihon Spring, and being so close to the desert, a water source was important. In recent years, archaeologists have found huge stones dating from about 1,800 years before the time of Jesus. These stones are believed to be from fortifications that guarded the precious water source from marauders. A tunnel with steps leading down to the spring dates to these same ancient times and can still be seen in Jerusalem today.

With water came people. Fourteen hundred years before the Common Era (which begins with the birth of Jesus), Jerusalem was a city. Pieces of clay cuneiform tablets, an early form of writing, show the ruler of Jerusalem writing to the Egyptian pharaoh asking for his help in putting down an uprising. (We don't have the return "mail," so we don't know if help was given or not.) Excavations have shown that from 1400 to 1200 BCE, Jerusalem was growing, with houses built on stone terraces and walls that may have been as high as thirty-three feet protecting the city.

Remains of a massive stone tower built about 1800 BCE to guard a pool near the Gihon Spring—part of ancient Jerusalem's water system.

Stone steps and a supporting wall built around the time of King David, approximately 1000 BCE.

Though archaeology gives us glimpses of the city during this period, the Bible does not mention Jerusalem. It is telling other stories about the descendants of Abraham—the people who would come to be known as Israelites, Hebrews, or Jews. When there was a drought in Canaan, the Israelites were forced to leave and travel to Egypt in search of food. There they prospered at first, but eventually their numbers grew to the point where the Egyptians became alarmed. Though these descendants of Abraham had once been welcomed in Egypt, now they were enslaved. To cut their numbers, Pharaoh, the Egyptian ruler, ordered that all male babies born to Hebrew families be drowned in the River Nile. But one baby was saved by Pharaoh's daughter, and she named him Moses. Though Moses was raised as an Egyptian, he killed an Egyptian overseer he found whipping an Israelite slave. Moses had to flee for his life into the desert, where, according to the Bible, God appeared to him and told him to return to Egypt and tell Pharaoh, "Let my people go!" When Pharaoh refused to free the Israelites, Moses unleashed plagues on Egypt, culminating in the deaths of Egypt's firstborn sons. At last, Pharaoh was ready to allow the slaves their freedom. This story, known as the Exodus, is still memorialized during the Jewish holiday of Passover.

Once the Jews were free, as the biblical narrative describes, they wandered in the desert. Then, as the story continues, Moses climbed to the top of a mountain, communed with God, and descended holding stone tablets inscribed with a set of laws that his people were to live by: the Ten Commandments.

According to the Bible story, God told Moses he wanted a worthy home for these holy tablets. They were to be kept in an ark (a box, or chest) fashioned of wood from the acacia tree and then covered with gold. The size of this ark was given in biblical measurements called cubits. No one today is exactly sure how big a cubit was, but scholars think the box was about four feet long by two and a half feet wide, and almost three feet high. Two cherubim, a kind of angel, decorated the ark, one at each end, their wings touching across the ark's lid. These creatures are not the soft baby angels we think of today when we hear the word *cherub*, but fierce protectors, devoted to the Lord.

The ark, however, was more than just a box or chest to hold the tablets. The Jewish people believed it held the power of God. Because of this, their armies often carried it into battle by holding it on long poles that fit through golden rings on the sides of the ark.

Since the ark held the stone tablets inscribed with the Ten

Commandments, and because obeying the commandments was another promise (or covenant) between God and the Jewish people, the ark came to be called the Ark of the Covenant. Does that name sound familiar? Many people today recognize it from the Indiana Jones movie *Raiders of the Lost Ark*. Over the centuries, legends, books, and—more recently—movies have grown up around the ark and its mystical powers. But fanciful tales hardly do justice to the reverence the Jewish people felt for the ark and its contents, and the important role it played in Jewish life. One psalm (a psalm is a sacred song or prayer) called it God's might, "the ark of Your strength."

That psalm is said to have been written by another famous biblical figure, King David. And it is with David that Mount Moriah and its rocky top come back into the story.

Biblical scholars put the birth of David around 1040 BCE. Bible writings (and later commentary in the Muslim holy book, the Quran) were once the only source of information about David. But in 1993 archaeologists working in northern Israel discovered an inscribed stone, called a stele, that mentioned "the house of David." This was the first time a reference to David had been found outside religious writings. That stele, which most scholars agree is referencing a royal dynasty that began with David, is now on display in the Israel Museum in Jerusalem.

There are many heroes and villains in the Bible, but few of them seem as real and as human as King David. He was a superb warrior, a devoted friend, and a canny ruler. He was also a musician and a poet; another beautiful psalm attributed to David begins, "The Lord is my shepherd; I shall not want." But he was also ruthless. The Bible tells the story of how King David once sent a soldier to be killed in battle so that he could have the soldier's wife.

David first appears in the Bible as a shepherd boy, but he made his

A stone tablet inscribed in the Aramaic language, dating from approximately the ninth century BCE. The highlighted phrase reads "the house of David."

reputation at the court of King Saul, the first king of Israel. There, as a young man, he volunteered to take on one of the Philistine enemies, a giant named Goliath. In the dramatic Bible story, David and Goliath met in the Valley of Elah and with one stone from his slingshot, David felled Goliath and became a hero.

After Saul's death, David, now king, was able to unite the southern country where he lived, Judah (source of the word *Jew*), and the northern country of Israel, making them one kingdom. It was to be called Israel and its people Israelites. David then decided to put the capital city in a place almost directly in between the two former factions. David's eyes turned to Jerusalem.

It didn't bother a warrior like David that Jerusalem was already inhabited by a tribe called the Jebusites. It had everything he wanted: location, a water supply in the Gihon Spring, and a link to his ancestors Abraham and Jacob. The Jebusites were sure that they could defend their well-fortified city. They jeered at the Israelites, telling them, "Even the blind and the lame could turn you away!"

Unfortunately for the Jebusites, not even their army could withstand the Israelite soldiers. In about 1000 BCE, after a fierce fight, David made the city of Jerusalem his own.

What was Jerusalem like? Historians estimate that it was then a city of perhaps 2,000 people. It had military buildings, a palace for its king, and houses for the local population. Rather than killing those people off, as often happened when a city was conquered, it seems the Israelites moved in alongside the Jebusites, who had their own gods.

But David wanted to make sure that the God of Israel had preeminence. One of the first things he did when he captured Jerusalem was to bring the Ark of the Covenant to its new home. The ark had been lodged in a town about ten miles from Jerusalem. Now David prepared a tent-shrine for the ark at the Gihon Spring, and, according to the biblical story, he led the procession as the sacred object was carried into Jerusalem. Wearing only a linen garment, the exuberant David danced and whirled in front of the ark as it entered the city amid much music and rejoicing.

Before long though, David had a realization. "Here I am, living in a house of cedar," he told the prophet Nathan, "while the ark of God remains in a tent."

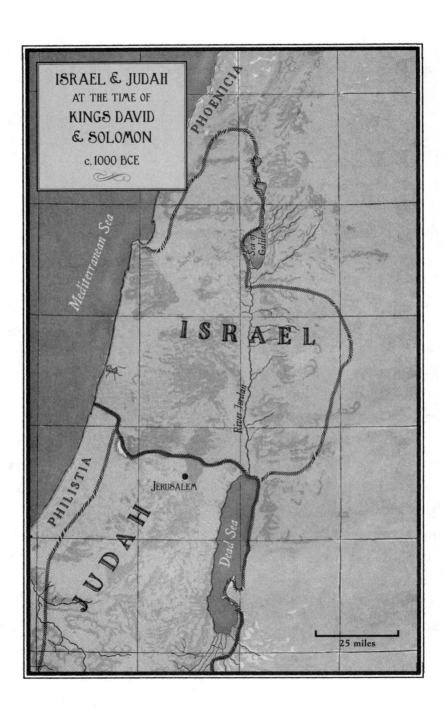

ISRAEL & JUDAH
AT THE TIME OF
KINGS DAVID
& SOLOMON

c. 1000 BCE

PHOENICIA

Mediterranean Sea

Sea of Galilee

I S R A E L

River Jordan

PHILISTIA

JERUSALEM

Dead Sea

J U D A H

25 miles

David and Nathan agreed that David should build a temple for the ark. However, according to the Bible, God said through his prophet Nathan that he did not want David to be the one to build the temple because he had shed too much blood. That job would have to wait for the right time and the right person.

The honor would go to David's son Solomon.

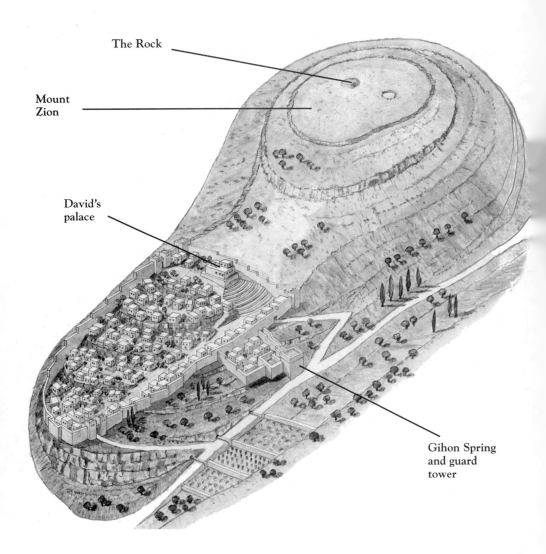

The Rock

Mount
Zion

David's
palace

Gihon Spring
and guard
tower

A reconstruction of how Jerusalem may have looked at the time
of King David.

2

SOLOMON'S TEMPLE

If David was disappointed that the Lord would not allow him to build a temple, the Bible doesn't mention it. What the Bible does say is that David took an active part in overseeing the preparations for construction while he was still alive.

The Bible describes how David went to the Jebusite king who had ruled over the city before it was taken by the Israelites and asked for the land atop the sacred mountain. Over the thousands of years since Abraham's time, Mount Moriah had taken on another name and was more commonly called Mount Zion. The king, who perhaps felt lucky to have been left alive after the battle, offered David this place as a gift, but David insisted on paying him fifty pieces of silver.

Then, according to the Bible, David busied himself drawing the plans for the temple, under the direction of God. He asked Hiram, king of Tyre, for cedarwood, and he gathered stone and stonecutters, gold, silver, and artisans to erect and beautify the building. Before David died—scholars place this event in biblical history in about 970 BCE—he entrusted his son Solomon with beginning the construction.

Solomon is another biblical figure who seems larger than life. He ruled over the united kingdoms of Israel and Judah, and under his reign the country became more powerful, with a strong army to protect it. Known far and wide for his wisdom, Solomon was often brought knotty problems to solve. The most famous was one concerning two women who each claimed the same baby as her own. How would Solomon decide who was telling the truth? After some thought, Solomon suggested cutting the child in two, giving each mother half. One woman was satisfied with this solution. The other was horrified. "Take him!" she cried. This declaration told Solomon all he needed to know. The real mother loved her child so much that she would hand him over to an impostor to save his life.

Solomon might have been best known for his wisdom, but he did not turn away from extravagance. His palace was filled with riches and decorated with the most opulent of luxuries, and it is reported in the Bible that he had hundreds of wives. Though Solomon's time was thousands of years ago, he has lived on in legends, literature, movies, music, and even manga.

The temple is said to have taken seven years to finish and to have been completed in the eleventh year of Solomon's reign, approximately 959 BCE. It was a magnificent structure, at least according to biblical descriptions. The temple itself was part of an enclosed compound that also housed Solomon's lavish palace. The long, narrow temple building was not particularly large. Because the biblical description is given in cubits, estimates of the size vary, but the dimensions of the temple are suggested to have been about a hundred and eighty feet long, ninety feet wide, and fifty feet high. It was surrounded by a courtyard and had three parts: a porch, a main hall, and a small, secluded area: the Holy of Holies.

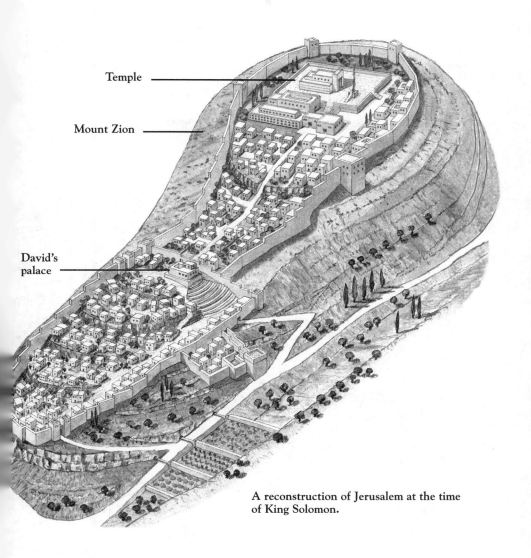

Temple

Mount Zion

David's palace

A reconstruction of Jerusalem at the time of King Solomon.

Several unusual objects stood in the courtyard. A huge basin of water resting on twelve bronze cattle was important symbolically, as were so many things in the temple. Some scholars think the water was a reminder of the chaos from which God formed the universe. Others think it represented the flowing waters of the Garden of Eden. It may also have been a symbol of the tranquil water of the world to come. The courtyard was probably as far into the temple as

SOLOMON'S TEMPLE
c. 959 BCE

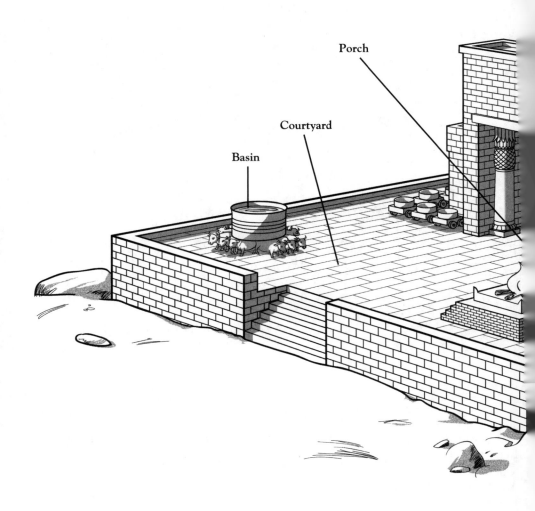

Porch

Courtyard

Basin

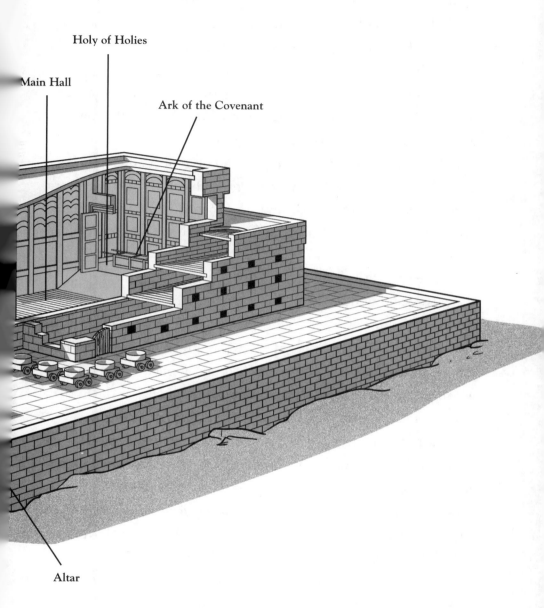

Holy of Holies

Main Hall

Ark of the Covenant

Altar

ordinary people were allowed to come, and it was there that they would have brought sacrifices to the Lord. If you were a priest or a member of royalty, you could have moved into the porch and the main hall.

The porch's entrance was flanked by two tall bronze pillars decorated with carved lilies and pomegranates. Two doors, made of juniper wood and decorated with angels and flowers, protected a long hall, twice as long as the porch. The hall housed two large golden candlesticks; a golden table for showbread, a flatbread meant as an offering to the Lord; and an incense altar of gold-plated cedar. The walls, also featuring flower carvings, were covered in gold.

At the end of the hall, a short staircase led to the Holy of Holies, a small space that held the Ark of the Covenant, which was hidden behind a curtain of blue, crimson, and purple linen. Walled with gold, the room was dominated by two powerful angelic figures. Facing each other, their wingtips touched and formed an arch under which the ark sat. The only person allowed to step inside the Holy of Holies was the Jewish high priest.

Most of the information we have about the temple—and, for that matter, about Solomon himself—comes from the Bible. The political and religious rivalries of recent times, to be discussed later in this book, have prevented almost any archaeological excavations from taking place on the Mount itself since the 1800s. There have been archaeological excavations around the Mount, as well as finds that came when nearby areas for public use were strengthened or repaired. Archaeologists are also sifting through stone and dirt removed in a 2005 renovation. These excavations have caused tensions

Remains of a temple in Ain Dara, Syria, that was similar in layout to Solomon's Temple, based on descriptions in the Hebrew Bible.

in modern-day Israel between Muslims and Jews, who both have strong feelings about the Jewish temple's past and present.

But despite there being little archaeological evidence, there are indications that Solomon's Temple did exist. For one thing, other ancient temples have been excavated in the Middle East that are very similar to the descriptions of Solomon's Temple in the Bible. One of these, Ain Dara, discovered in Syria, caused excitement among scholars when it was excavated in the 1980s, in part because of its similarity to the descriptions of Solomon's Temple. Although it was built around three hundred years before Solomon's Temple and was not dedicated to the Hebrew God, it is on a high hill, overlooking the city; its design, with three rooms, is the same; and pieces of floral carvings have been found. In fact, about half the elements of Solomon's Temple, as described in the Bible, are the same as those at Ain Dara. This means that while we have no similar archaeological proof of the existence of Solomon's Temple, other finds from around the same time confirm what temples of the era looked like.

Another thing that points to the existence of Solomon's Temple is the way later writers discuss it. In sections of the Jewish Bible called Kings, which describe events that took place about a hundred years after the reign of Solomon, references are made to repairing the temple. There are a few sentences about someone hiding in the temple; still another section mentions gold being ripped out of the temple to pay back a debt to the king of Assyria. None of this is proof, but it seems odd that these casual mentions would be made if there was no temple.

In 2003, a discovery was made that seemed to confirm the existence of Solomon's Temple. A private antiquities collector in Israel came into possession of a carved stone, about as big as a piece of letter-size paper, that talks about repairs to the temple. It is very much the same as the discussion of temple repairs in the Book of Kings. Named the Jehoash Stone, for the prince who executed the repairs, it has caused controversy among historians and archaeologists, who have tangled over whether the stone is authentic or a forgery, with scholars on both sides of the issue.

Whatever the facts about Solomon's Temple, its importance for the Jewish people and the evolution of religious thought remains. The temple was a symbol of many things: the growing importance of the Jewish kingdom, the joining of political and religious life, and a visible affirmation of the Jewish people's relationship with their God.

The temple in Jerusalem was also different from other temples and altars throughout the ancient world. Pagan temples were places to worship gods or goddesses whose images or statues could be seen or touched. But the second of the Ten Commandments insists that the Jewish people not make any likenesses for their temple. Worshippers could not look at the face of God in statues or pictures, but in the holiness of the temple, they could still experience the divine presence.

Solomon, however, did seem to think the temple was going to be a home for God in a very real way. At the temple's dedication, the Bible quotes him as saying, "I have indeed built you an exalted house, a place for you to dwell in forever."

THE FALL—AND RISE—
OF THE TEMPLE

Eternal means forever. Jews will forever associate the mountain where the temple was built with their God. But as for Solomon's Temple, that stood for only about 350 years.

Solomon, for all his virtues as a king, had faults as well. The biblical narrative describes how he favored southern Judaea, where his family was from, over northern Israel. He taxed Israel more heavily and conscripted more soldiers from the north. The united kingdom began to show strains. After Solomon's death, his son, Rehoboam, became king. He demanded even more money from Israel, the rift became permanent, and Judaea and Israel separated around 930 BCE.

The temple remained in Jerusalem, in the Judaean kingdom. Nine years into Rehoboam's reign, Judaea was attacked by Egypt's pharaoh, Shishak I, who also invaded Israel. An inscription on a court wall, discovered in Karnak in Upper Egypt, celebrates Shishak and names several of the towns that he plundered and defeated. The next centuries were a continual parade of battles, alliances, and betrayals in both Judaea and Israel, during which the temple's riches were often looted—sometimes taken in battle, sometimes used for ransom or bribes by a succession of Judaea's kings.

At the same time, ideas about worship, God, and what He wanted were also evolving. Originally, the Jewish God was thought to be Lord over only His people. There were hundreds, if not thousands of other gods in the region, and often their worship commingled. But the idea began to slowly grow—at least among the Jews—that their God was not just superior to other gods, He should be the only God to be worshipped. This was a new, even startling way of thinking.

There was also another strain of thought that was flourishing in the eighth and seventh centuries before the Common Era, which said worship was supposed to be more than just bringing animal

A stone relief from the city of Nimrud in ancient Assyria (now in Iraq), dated about 865 BCE, shows Assyrian soldiers attacking the walls of a fortified city.

Photos show the excavation of the ancient city of Babylon and a mosaic of a lion from the city's Ishtar Gate, built by King Nebuchadnezzar II in the sixth century BCE.

sacrifices to God. What God really wanted was social justice. He wanted the poor to be fed, and care to be given to widows and orphans.

In 772 BCE, disaster befell the northern kingdom of Israel. The Assyrian empire invaded and destroyed the country. Some people were able to flee, and many went to Judaea, so the southern kingdom grew in size. Then, almost two hundred years later, in 597 BCE, it was Judaea's turn to be invaded by a mighty foe. Nebuchadnezzar II, a powerful Babylonian king with a strong army, seized Jerusalem. Unlike many people mentioned in the Bible, the record on Nebuchadnezzar is clear: he is a historical figure. There are firsthand accounts of his reign, and his name is mentioned on artifacts. Still, almost all of what we know of his invasions of Jerusalem comes from Jewish religious writings.

Nebuchadnezzar carried off Jerusalem's treasures and Judaea's most important citizens: royalty, priests, and artisans. Thousands of people—perhaps as many as 10,000—were forced to relocate to Babylon, about five hundred miles away. But despite Jerusalem being a shell of its former self, there were rebellions against Babylonian rule for almost a decade. In 589 BCE, Nebuchadnezzar had had enough, and began another invasion. After a siege of approximately thirty months, on the ninth day of the Jewish month of Av in 586 BCE, Babylonian soldiers swarmed into Jerusalem, looting and burning the city and destroying its most important place, the temple.

The biblical prophet Jeremiah, who is considered to be the author of the Book of Lamentations, describes the suffering in vivid words. The word lamentation means wild, uncontrollable grief, and Jeremiah frames Jerusalem as a weeping widow, bereft because her children have been taken into captivity. He recounts the horror of seeing the devastated city and talks about the temple, now in ruins: "The stones of the sanctuary are poured out in the top of every street."

And what of the Ark of the Covenant, which had resided in the temple's Holy of Holies? After the temple's destruction by the Babylonians, that precious artifact was gone. Some stories say it was buried by priests under the temple's stone floor, its raging power a death sentence for anyone who tried to find it. Others think it is in a cave outside Jerusalem, to be left undiscovered until a time of God's choosing. There's a legend that the Knights Templar discovered it in Jerusalem during the Middle Ages and spirited it into hiding. One contemporary theory even puts the ark with the Lemba tribe in Zimbabwe. And, of course, if you believe the ending of the movie *Raiders of the Lost Ark*, it's in a warehouse in Washington, D.C.

In fact, most historians think the ark was simply carried off by the Babylonians, or destroyed along with the temple. Whatever its fate,

A stone relief from the city of Nineveh, dating from approximately 700 BCE, shows Babylonian prisoners playing musical instruments.

An inscribed stone cylinder dating from 536 BCE includes a reference to King Cyrus's decree allowing Jews to return to Jerusalem.

the legend of the Ark of the Covenant has never died and sparks imaginations even today.

The Jews were exiled in Babylonia for almost sixty years, though a small group remained in Jerusalem, trying to eke out a living. The exiles, ironically, were the ones who had much better lives. They were treated well by their captors, and in many ways were able to integrate into Babylonian society. Still, Jerusalem, or Zion, as it is sometimes more poetically called, tugged at their hearts. With the ark gone and the temple burned, its remaining stones hacked to the ground, the Jews—those still at home and those in exile—had to come to terms with the reality that they were now without their most sacred place. How were they to worship? Some of the most haunting words in the Bible come in Psalm 137: "By the rivers of Babylon, there we sat down, yea, we wept, when we remembered Zion."

By 538 BCE, Babylonia's fortunes, and the fortunes of the Jews living there, were about to change. Babylonia had been conquered by Persia, and its king, Cyrus, made the displaced Jews an offer: they could go back to Jerusalem and rebuild their temple. Some of the

Jews stayed where they had made new lives, but others, more than 40,000 of them according to the Bible, returned. The first thing they did was set up an altar where the temple had stood. The Jews of Jerusalem could once more make sacrifices to their Lord.

The temple rebuilding project progressed slowly. Maybe it was political squabbles; maybe those returning were too poor to do much building. But finally, in 515 BCE, more than twenty years after the return, a new temple was completed.

The builders of this Second Temple did their best. They imported what cedarwood they could from Lebanon; they may even have had some gold and silver they had been allowed to bring back with them from Babylon. But one biblical writer wasn't impressed. Upon seeing the rebuilt temple he asked, "Who is left among you who saw this house in its former glory? How do you see it now? Is it not as nothing in your eyes?"

What this new temple lacked in beauty, it made up for in sturdiness, lasting more than four hundred years. As Jerusalem grew into an important city again, foreign powers eyed it with interest once more.

The first to capture Jerusalem in this Second Temple period was Alexander the Great. Alexander is a fascinating historical figure and one of the greatest generals the world has ever seen. Only sixteen years old when he took over the Greek throne in 336 BCE, he inherited a strong kingdom and a fierce fighting army. By the time he died at age thirty-two, he had conquered Syria and Egypt and overturned the powerful Persian empire, spreading Greek culture throughout the Middle East. In 332 BCE, Jerusalem and its temple came under his rule.

Alexander didn't live long enough to put his imprint on Jerusalem and the surrounding countryside of Judaea, but the area's strategic location put it in the center of fighting between the Ptolemies and the Seleucids, two of the three Greek dynasties that carved up Alexander's empire after his death from illness in 323 BCE.

The Ptolemies, though Greek, were centered in Egypt, and the rulers called themselves pharaohs. They took control of Judaea soon after Alexander's death and were impressed with the Jewish religion. Tradition says that sometime in the third century BCE the ruler Ptolemy II started the translation of the Hebrew Bible into Greek, which was the common language of the day throughout the region.

The pharaohs' interest in Judaism did not always serve them well, however. According to biblical reports, around 221 BCE one of the Ptolemy kings, Ptolemy IV, decided to take a closer look at the temple. He told his hosts that he wanted to step inside the Holy of Holies, which was still the most sacred part of the temple, even though the ark was long gone. The temple priests told him no. Ptolemy went in anyway, much to the consternation of both the priests and the people of Jerusalem. Legend has it that he immediately fell ill and had to be pulled out of the sacred spot by his bodyguards.

When the Seleucids rousted the Ptolemies from Jerusalem in 198 BCE, the temple fell into their hands. At first, the Seleucids seemed to revere the temple and paid to fix the damages it had incurred during the battle between themselves and the Ptolemies. The temple was beautified and fortified, and a good drainage system was put in place so that the blood from all the sacrificed animals wouldn't pollute the temple grounds.

But in 176 BCE, a Seleucid king, out of cash for fighting his wars, came up with the idea of raiding the temple's coffers. Not only did they contain gold and silver, but there were also donations and funds set aside for widows and orphans. The king sent a high-ranking minister to steal the temple's treasure, but, according to the story, God intervened with a physical punishment so severe the minister returned empty-handed and told the king the next time he wanted someone to plunder the temple, he should send somebody else.

Not long after, another Seleucid king, Antiochus IV, insisted that the Jews turn their backs on what was holy to them and worship the Greek gods. Then, deciding that he himself was a god, Antiochus ordered the people to worship him! The Jews of Judaea were both furious and frightened. One group of Jews called the Maccabees, who were living in the countryside, rebelled with a ragtag group of soldiers and over time fought down the king's powerful army. But when the Maccabees reached the temple in Jerusalem in 164 BCE, they found that the Greek soldiers had defiled it. Statues of Greek gods and goddesses desecrated even the holiest spots. Jewish law forbade Jews from eating pork, and seeing pig blood smeared on the altar was particularly loathsome to the Maccabees. Meanwhile, the menorah, the seven-branched candleholder meant to burn with eternal light, stood dark and neglected.

The Maccabees scrubbed and cleaned the temple and built a new altar, but when they went to light the menorah so they could have a rededication ceremony, they could find only a small vial of oil to burn, hardly enough for one day. Yet as the story of Hanukkah—told in the Jewish writings 1 and 2 Maccabees—relates, the menorah lights kept burning for eight days until new holy oil could be found.

For approximately the next 150 years, descendants of the Maccabees, now called the Hasmoneans, ruled the country and ruled the temple, which became the centerpiece of an expanded Jewish state. Rituals and laws were more closely observed. Animal sacrifices continued to be a large part of temple activities.

Some Jews didn't like the ways the laws were being interpreted by the priests and broke away from the temple. Others were angry that their country, over the decades, had taken on some of the attributes of Greek culture, for instance an emphasis on athletics. But for the most part, the temple's influence on the Jewish people only grew stronger.

Then, in the last decades before the Common Era, a new king appeared on the scene. He decided to make the temple much larger, more beautiful, and more influential than even the Jews, with all their reverence for that holy place, could have believed.

The Jewish world was about to meet Herod the Great.

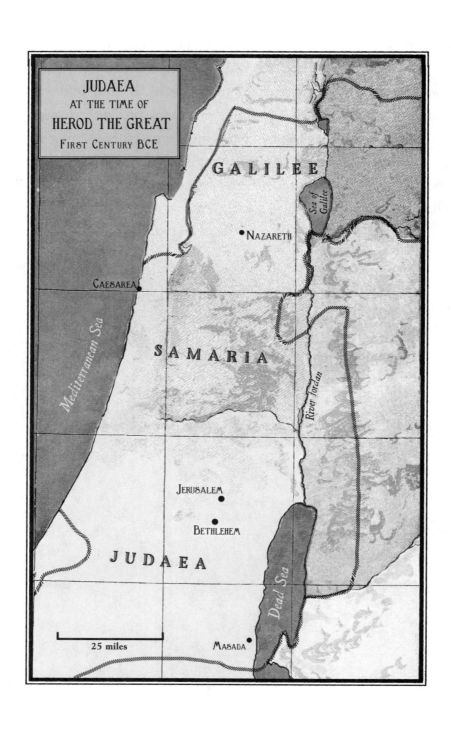

JUDAEA
AT THE TIME OF
HEROD THE GREAT
FIRST CENTURY BCE

GALILEE

Sea of Galilee

• NAZARETH

CAESAREA •

Mediterranean Sea

SAMARIA

River Jordan

JERUSALEM
•

• BETHLEHEM

JUDAEA

Dead Sea

25 miles

MASADA •

HEROD'S TEMPLE

Powerful Herod wasn't called "the Great" because of his good qualities. He was a wily manipulator who murdered those who got in his way, including his closest relatives.

Herod's family hadn't always been Jewish. Born in around 73 BCE, he came from Idumaea, a land south of Judaea that had been captured by the Hasmoneans about fifty years earlier. To fit in better with their Jewish rulers, the family converted to Judaism.

This was a turbulent time in the lands around the Mediterranean Sea. Civil war had broken out among the Hasmoneans in 76 BCE. It ended when Rome took over Judaea and its capital, Jerusalem, in 63 BCE. The Roman Empire was expanding and gobbling up the territory around the Mediterranean. Herod's father aligned himself with Julius Caesar, who had come out on top in a Roman civil war. Caesar made Herod's father governor of Judaea in 47 BCE, and he in turn appointed Herod, a young man in his twenties, governor of Galilee, an area north of Judaea, and, according to the Bible, the place where Jesus grew up.

Four short years later, Herod's father was assassinated and Herod became governor of Judaea. In 39 BCE, in recognition of his loyalty to Rome, he was appointed king of Judaea. A clever politician, Herod skillfully befriended the powerful in Rome. Despite having ultimate authority, the Roman government knew that it was best if a Jewish king, who understood the country's customs and constituents, ruled—as long as his loyalty was to Rome.

Herod was a busy man. He spent considerable effort throughout his thirty-three-year reign staying on the right side of Roman rulers as one after another was toppled. He killed his half brother, mother-in-law, and even his wife and several of his sons, all to keep his power. But as brutal as Herod was, he is also remembered for his impressive building projects, which changed the landscape of Judaea.

To honor his Roman patrons and as a gift to his pagan subjects, in 22 BCE, Herod began building the city of Caesarea on the shores of the Mediterranean. It developed into a vibrant town with a temple to the Roman gods, a stadium for chariot races, and a large amphitheater. Its ruins, located between the modern cities of Tel Aviv and Haifa, can still be seen by tourists today. But even that ambitious project paled beside what Herod had planned for Jerusalem.

By Herod's time, Jerusalem was once more a dynamic and flourishing city. Population estimates range from about 50,000 to 100,000 residents, most of them Jews, but there were non-Jews as well, including contingents of Roman soldiers.

The city was divided into a lower and an upper section. The crowded lower section was home to poorer folk as well as to what could be called a middle class, made up of merchants and craftspeople—weavers, carpenters, and metalworkers. Limestone dwellings, crowded next to one another on dusty streets, each housed several generations. Wealthier families made their homes in the airier upper section. The walls of their spacious rooms were decorated with tile mosaics and painted frescoes of fruits and flowers. Archaeologists have found—and continue to find—rooms of these homes, almost intact, that can be visited in Jerusalem today.

Remains of a house in Jerusalem built in the first century BCE, including a fine mosaic floor.

The numbers of people in Jerusalem swelled during Jewish feast holidays such as Passover, when thousands, even hundreds of thousands of Jews from the surrounding areas—and much farther—would visit the temple to celebrate and make sacrifices. Sacrifice was still an essential part of temple life. Animal sacrifice seems cruel, even shocking, to us today, but it was common throughout the ancient world. For important holidays like Passover, Jewish visitors to the temple were required to provide a lamb, though the poor might bring birds. Throughout the year, men and women also visited the temple to make sacrificial offerings in the hope of forgiveness of sins or to show thankfulness for blessings in their lives.

The temple was the focus of Jewish worship. So when, in 20 BCE, in the eighteenth year of his reign, Herod announced a rebuilding of the temple and expansion plans for the area around it, the citizens were worried. Jerusalem had seen more than its share of hostilities over the years, and, of course, the temple had been destroyed once already by Babylonia. Tensions between the Jews and their Roman overlords, and on occasion between Jews themselves, were always bubbling just below the surface. How could the Jews of Jerusalem be sure that Herod's project would not be stopped midstream by war or rebellion? What if the old temple was demolished before a new one could be built? Could the Jewish people survive another tragedy surrounding the temple?

Herod had an answer to those questions. He vowed that he would not start rebuilding the temple until every piece was in place for its successor. As the ancient historian Josephus, who was alive at the time, reports, Herod gathered thousands of wagons, hired 10,000 skilled workers, and found a thousand priests who could be trained to build the holiest parts of the temple, which required sanctified hands. (It must be noted, however, that Josephus did have a tendency to exaggerate.)

The reconstruction of the temple and an expansion of the site was a monumental undertaking. In fact, it would go on for decades, even after Herod's death, although reportedly the work on the temple building itself was finished in less than two years.

The first thing Herod's architects and builders had to do was something that sounds simple, but wasn't. They needed to construct a level surface on which the temple and other structures would stand. This platform would be held up by walls that Josephus called "the greatest ever seen by man." They were certainly massive. Made of limestone from nearby quarries, most of the blocks weighed between

Part of the temple wall. The huge, neatly fitted stone blocks on the lower left were placed during the rebuilding and expansion of the temple under Herod the Great. The looser, uneven stones on the lower right are from an earlier period.

two and five tons. Some weighed as much as fifty tons, and a few were even heavier. These blocks were cut so well that they fit together perfectly, with no need for mortar to cement them.

Inside the walls, the platform was also held up by a series of vaulted archways that centuries later was given the whimsical name Solomon's Stables, as though King Solomon had put his horses there during the First Temple period. The spaces formed by the archways are actually believed to have been storage areas, and were of course built long after Solomon's time.

Herod's workmen used ingenious building techniques to expand the platform. According to one modern-day analysis, it was enlarged by pouring fill material at the same time the walls were being constructed. "Thus, the first course of stones was laid in the valley surrounding the previous Temple Mount. Then the area between the new and old walls was filled up to the level of the top of this course." This process continued until the new platform was as high as the previous one, but twice the size in width. Now there was a flat surface on which to begin. The platform was the base for the huge complex that was to be built next. Just consider the size of the Temple Mount. In today's terms, it was the size of more than twenty football fields. The temple building itself was just one part of the temple expanse, and rather a small one, really; it had to maintain the measurements that were given in the Bible. But there were no rules about how large and grand everything surrounding it could be, and that was where Herod's architects and builders could construct their glorious vision.

The Temple Mount had to fulfill two very different roles. One was as a commercial and administrative center. On the southern side of the platform was a three-aisled structure called the Royal Stoa. Open on one side, it was held up by rows of columns, each column so wide, one historian of the time wrote, that it would take three men holding hands to surround it. The stoa itself, according to archaeologists, was more than thirty feet tall and almost eight hundred feet long. The building had all sorts of practical purposes. It housed government offices, a bank for changing money, and a market. It also served as the meeting place of the Sanhedrin, the supreme religious body of Israel. Since the Temple Mount was also a gathering place for teachers and students, there were areas for study, inside and out.

Herod, ever wary of attacks from without and within his kingdom, also built a fortress adjacent to the northwestern corner of the Mount, a place to house watchful soldiers. He named the fortress Antonia, after his Roman patron, Mark Antony.

But commerce, study, and security were not the focal points of the Temple Mount. As the symbolic place where God resides, the whole Temple Mount area had a second, higher purpose. It was meant to inspire awe in the people who approached it, to give them a sense of the radiance of their Lord. In this, the material used for the temple building itself contributed significantly. The marble used had a lustrous sheen that gave the building an almost otherworldly glow. Where limestone was used, it was covered with gold.

Limestone and even marble, however, are only building materials. Herod's architects designed the Temple Mount to make it an experience. Every step the multitude of the visitors took led upward, as if the continuous climbing toward the temple were a journey to heaven itself.

Visitors who flocked through one of the several gates around the Mount area found themselves in dark tunnels ending in staircases that led up to daylight. Arriving on the Temple Mount, they found

One of the main entrance stairways to the temple built under Herod.

themselves in a busy, lively area called the Court of the Gentiles, bounded on the south side by the stoa. The court was like a noisy bazaar where all sorts of commercial transactions took place: money changing, the purchase of animals for sacrifice, of food and drink, even of souvenirs. The term *gentile* means anyone who is not Jewish, and the court was the one area of the Temple Mount anyone could visit. However, gentiles were allowed no farther. Archaeologists have found signs carved in stone in both Latin and Greek that sternly warn of the consequences: NO FOREIGNER IS TO ENTER WITHIN THE BALUSTRADE AND EMBANKMENT AROUND THE SANCTUARY. WHOEVER IS CAUGHT WILL HAVE HIMSELF TO BLAME FOR HIS DEATH WHICH FOLLOWS.

A stone from the balustrade surrounding the temple with an inscription in Greek warning non-Jews against entering.

Other activities went on around the Court of the Gentiles, too. For Jews who had to purify themselves before moving to the inner courtyards, there were ritual baths, or *mikvahs*, for their use.

An ancient *mikvah,* or ritual bath. This one was excavated just outside the Temple Mount; similar baths were inside the temple courtyards.

The temple building was always visible, gleaming in the sun, but to reach it, Jews next entered the Court of the Women. It was a joyous place where music and dancing were encouraged in praise of the Lord. Despite its name, both men and women were allowed there, but while men could move closer to the temple, females could go no farther.

Moving up several feet led to an area known as the Court of the Israelites. From this vantage point Jewish men could observe through a narrow space the priests, a bit higher up, performing sacrifices at the Court of the Priests. That was where the actual work of sacrifice—preparing the animals, making burnt offerings, and then cleansing the area—took place.

Finally, the journey toward God ended at the spacious temple courtyard surrounded by imposing columns. In the center, twelve steps led to the handsome temple building itself. No detail had been

HEROD'S TEMPLE
First Century CE

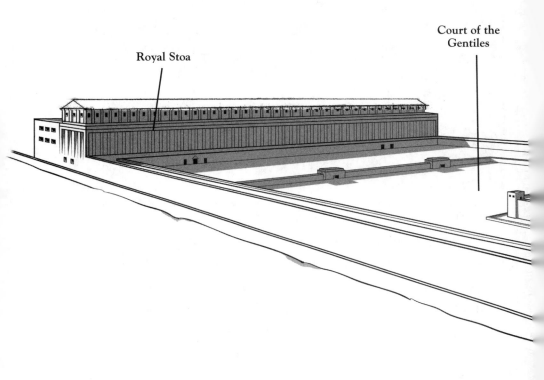

Royal Stoa

Court of the
Gentiles

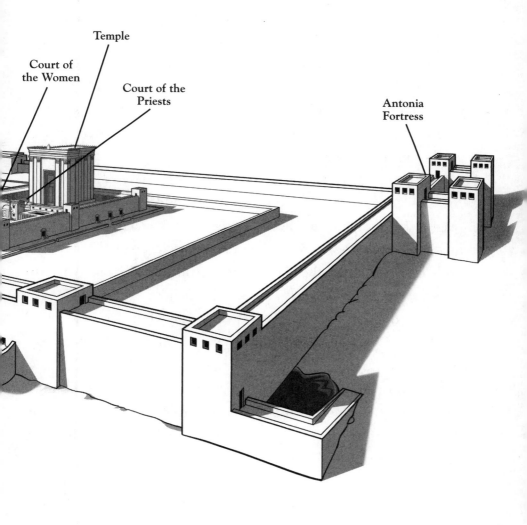

Court of
the Women

Temple

Court of the
Priests

Antonia
Fortress

overlooked to ensure the temple's sanctity. There were even spikes placed around the top of the building to keep birds from landing and despoiling it with droppings.

The temple building had the same dimensions as the previous temples. Its large doorway, seventy feet high, opened into a porch-like room, called the *ulam*. Behind the *ulam* was the main sanctuary, through which the priests, the only men allowed this close to the temple, entered. On each side of the doors were columns as tall as a man and decorated with flowers entwined with grapevines. Inside the sanctuary, just as in Solomon's Temple, there were twelve loaves of showbread and a menorah.

Then—the Holy of Holies. There was only one way into the innermost sanctuary, past two curtains beautifully embroidered with eagles and lions, and, as always, there was only one person who was allowed inside, the high priest. Even he could enter the chamber only once a year, on the Day of Atonement, Yom Kippur, which to this day is the holiest day on the Jewish calendar.

What did the high priest see when he entered the Holy of Holies?

Walls of gold surrounding an empty chamber, built on a rock. Legend says it is the rock of Abraham, Jacob, and David.

Our knowledge of what the temple looked like comes from archaeologists, religious writers, and historians. Of the latter, the historian Josephus, who actually visited the temple, offers the most evocative descriptions: the temple "at the first rising of the sun, reflected back a fiery splendor, and made those who forced themselves to look upon it to turn their eyes away as they would have done to the sun's own rays." He says the temple gleamed so white that from a distance it looked like a mountain of snow.

The names of almost all the tens of thousands who must have

visited Herod's Temple are lost to history. But the names of one man, his family, and his followers have become entwined with the story of the temple. More than 2,000 years later, his name is still known all over the world: Jesus of Nazareth.

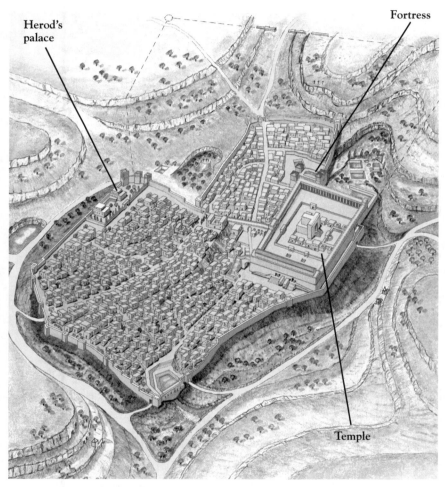

A reconstruction of Jerusalem at the time of Herod shows the new temple dominating the city, the Roman fortress at its northwest corner, and Herod's palace to the west.

JESUS AT THE TEMPLE

For pilgrims coming to visit the temple from outside Jerusalem, the journey was usually a joyous affair, with family and friends often traveling together. According to the Gospel of Luke in the New Testament of the Bible, one of those family groups included a couple named Mary and Joseph and their son, Jesus.

Jesus's first trip to the temple came when he was just an infant. Luke's gospel says that, forty days after Jesus's birth, Mary and Joseph took their son to Jerusalem, where, as was the custom, he was presented at the temple and a sacrifice of two turtledoves was made.

When Jesus was twelve, Luke writes, Mary and Joseph brought him to the temple once more, this time to celebrate Passover. After the festival was over, Mary and Joseph returned to their caravan for the trip home thinking Jesus was with them, but the boy had remained behind. Realizing that their son was missing, they rushed back to the temple area, only to find him sitting with learned rabbis, the teachers of the day, listening, asking questions, and impressing his elders with his understanding and wisdom.

The birth of Jesus coincided with a particularly tumultuous time in Jewish history. Approximately four years before the birth of Jesus, a sickly Herod was nearing the end of his days. One of his final acts was to place a golden eagle at an entrance gate to the temple. The eagle was a symbol of Rome and of its power over Judaea. This insult infuriated the Jewish population. Two rabbis encouraged a crowd of young men to climb the gate and remove the eagle. They hacked it down, but were quickly captured. A dying Herod watched as the men were punished by being burned alive.

Only days before his death around 4 BCE, Herod murdered the son who was supposed to rule after him. His three remaining sons were weak, and Rome soon saw that none of them could take Herod's place. Eventually, in 26 CE, they gave the job of prefect, or governor, of Judaea to one of their own, Pontius Pilate.

Meanwhile, after Herod's death, the unrest continued. The people of Judaea hoped for a Jewish Messiah ("anointed one") to come from God and free them from the burden of Roman rule. Into this cauldron of hope, fear, and desperation came Jesus of Nazareth, who, according to biblical time lines, began his public ministry around the age of thirty. The New Testament describes Jesus as an intense and charismatic preacher, a man of miracles who captivated crowds with his calls for repentance and lessons in how to live. Jesus's preaching about the world to come suggested to some that he might be the longed-for Messiah.

Jesus and his followers were only one group among several very different strains of Judaism vying for their fellow countrymen's attention and support, and even those strands could be mixed up and intertwined.

The Sadducees were what you might call the establishment. Many were priests. They were in charge of maintaining temple rites, and they worked with their Roman overseers to make sure things ran smoothly in Jerusalem. The historian Josephus reports that the Sadducees—the elite—were not held in high favor by the average citizen, who preferred the Pharisees and their more accessible interpretation of Jewish scripture.

The Pharisees led a popular political movement that held more flexible ideas about Judaism. They emphasized teaching, and often explained the Torah, the first five books of the Jewish Bible, by telling stories.

Holding a different view of the temple entirely were the Essenes. This was the group that is believed to have written the Dead Sea Scrolls, one of the greatest archaeological finds of modern times. Discovered in 1947 in clay pots and scattered through a honeycomb of limestone caves near the Dead Sea, these scrolls tell us much about first-century life, as well as about the Essenes themselves.

The Essenes had turned their backs on the temple in Jerusalem. As far as they were concerned, the priests in charge were corrupt, were in league with the Romans, and had defiled the temple beyond use. They awaited the coming of a Messiah, or perhaps two, who would inaugurate a new era.

Finally, there were the Zealots, who were less concerned with religion and more interested in revolution. They despised the Romans and the chokehold they had over their country's day-to-day life. They wanted to incite rebellion against Rome and expel its soldiers from their land.

In ways big and small, all of these groups played roles in the life of Jesus. Though critical of the Pharisees in biblical accounts, he also held some of the same views, including belief in an afterlife and the idea of treating others as one wishes to be treated oneself. And Jesus, like the Pharisees, told stories, or parables, to his followers to make the ways of God come alive. Like the Zealots, he sought a new kingdom for Israel, though from his teachings it appears he thought this was to come through spiritual change, not actual rebellion. The writings of the Essenes seem to have shaped some of the beliefs of Jesus's cousin John the Baptist, who cleansed people of their sins in the River Jordan and influenced Jesus's own teachings. As for the Sadducees, it was members of their highest court, known as the Sanhedrin, who played a part in Jesus's death.

The gospels report that much of Jesus's time was spent close to home in Galilee, north of Jerusalem. But there are also events in his adulthood, just as in his childhood, that tie him closely to the temple in Jerusalem. He preached there, attracting crowds and upsetting the establishment priests with his talk of how the Kingdom of God was at hand.

Perhaps the most famous of these events is Jesus's furious encounter with those who changed foreign money so visitors could buy things at the temple. It is reported in all four of the gospels—Matthew, Mark, Luke, and John—and, in the first three, is described as happening during the last week of Jesus's life. Though there are differences in the tellings, the gospels agree that the incident took place around Passover, when the Temple Mount was crowded with thousands of visitors.

The temple did not seem like a holy place to Jesus at the moment he walked into the bazaars along the Court of the Gentiles. The focus was not on prayer, but on buying and selling. Making a short whip from cords, Jesus charged toward the money changers and overturned their tables. "My house shall be called the house of prayer," he told them furiously, "but you have made it a den of thieves!"

This dramatic display must have chilled the Sanhedrin. Jesus was roiling up the people. He had been speaking against the establishment and offering fresh ways of thinking about earth and heaven. A growing number of Jews believed he was the Messiah.

The Sanhedrin realized something had to be done about Jesus. It was their job to keep order in the city, to make sure that the crowds did not get out of hand. There had been a riot after Herod's death in which 3,000 Jews had died. Restless Jerusalem was often close to explosion. Jesus, with his bold speech and actions, seemed to be a match that could light the fuse.

The story of Jesus's last days, the Easter story, is one of the best known in the world. After a meal referred to as the Last Supper, Jesus was betrayed by his friend and disciple Judas. Jesus was arrested and questioned by members of the Sanhedrin as to who he believed himself to be, but they got no real answers. Under Roman law, the Sanhedrin didn't have the power to execute anyone, so they referred his case to Pontius Pilate.

Pilate is known from historical writings to have been a no-nonsense administrator with a cruel streak. The accusation against Jesus was that he was seen as some sort of king of the Jews, and that was a direct threat to Rome's authority in Judaea. Pilate sentenced him to death by crucifixion—being hung from or, as in Jesus's case, nailed to a cross. A particularly painful and often slow way to die, crucifixion was an exclusively Roman form of execution.

After his death, Jesus's followers claimed that he rose from the dead, appeared to them, and ascended into heaven. And while this belief became the mystery from which Christianity began, it would be at least a hundred years before Christianity was universally regarded as a religion entirely separate from Judaism. In the first decades following Jesus's death, many people considered themselves simply Jewish followers of Jesus. Slowly, Christianity evolved, but it flourished mainly outside of Jerusalem. There were two reasons for this. First, there was the great success of the apostle Paul (also a Jew), who brought the gospels primarily to gentiles far from Jerusalem.

Second, there were cataclysmic events about to unfold in Jerusalem. Over the next decades, the tensions between the Jewish people and the Romans who ruled them would erupt into rioting, insurrection, destruction, and death.

6

DESTRUCTION

Almost forty years after Jesus's death, the glorious Temple Mount was a windswept mass of rubble. The golden decorations were gone. The luminous marble was in pieces, the massive limestone blocks hauled away to be used in other building projects. Without a temple, sacrifices were no more. And many of the Jewish people were dead or scattered.

Jerusalem was now, after 70 CE, just a skeleton of its former self.

How had this destruction of both a city and its temple happened? Herod's massive structure, one of the wonders of the ancient world, was supposed to last forever. Had God allowed the Romans to destroy the temple? That is the conclusion that some came to. Matthew's gospel in the New Testament reports that Jesus had said, the last time he was in the temple, "Do you see all these great buildings? Not one stone here will be left on another; every one will be thrown down."

Christians believe these are Jesus's words. But since the gospels were written decades after his death, some historians think this passage became part of the gospels because when they were being written the temple had already been destroyed.

After Jesus's death, in approximately 33 CE, Rome gradually tightened its grip on Judaea, leading to sporadic but intense uprisings by different segments of Jewish society, which, at various times, were also fighting with one another. Thousands of Jews—and Roman soldiers—were killed in these episodes of violence.

In 39 CE, the Roman emperor Caligula ordered that his statue be erected at the Jerusalem temple. The Jewish people considered this blasphemy. Tens of thousands of Jews—men, women, and children—gathered outside the sanctuary, ready to die before they would let this happen. They believed God would intervene. Then, whether or not it was God's doing, Caligula, back in Rome, was assassinated, and the plan was dropped.

A few years later, a jeering Roman soldier made an obscene gesture to the Jewish crowds gathered at the temple for the annual Passover celebration and a thousand more Jews were trampled to death in the ensuing melee.

The temple building itself, according to Josephus, had been completed in less than two years, but for much else—other buildings, fortifications—the work was still ongoing. It took approximately eighty years, until 64 CE, for the massive Temple Mount area that Herod the Great had envisioned to reach completion. It took much less time to fall.

The beginning of the end came in 66 CE. Florus, the Roman governor now in charge of Jerusalem, needed an influx of money and he knew where to look—in the temple treasury. The silver he commandeered came at a great price, however. A rebellion broke out and thousands of Jews were killed. The Zealots took command of the revolt, and even though some Jews wanted to keep the peace with Rome, it was not long before most of Jerusalem was under rebel control. After a legion of Roman soldiers was killed, Rome sent one of its best generals, Titus, to take back the city.

In the spring of the year 70, Titus began the siege of Jerusalem. Josephus, once a commander in the Jewish army, had switched his loyalties to Rome. An eyewitness to the events, he was even sent as a negotiator to persuade the Jewish fighters to surrender, to no avail. Josephus reports how the Romans stormed the walls of the Temple Mount with huge battering rams. First the northern wall, the most recently completed, was destroyed, and just a week later, the wall around the markets was demolished as well.

The battle lasted into the summer, when Roman troops broke into the inner courts. Titus had issued orders not to destroy the magnificent temple, but his soldiers disobeyed and set the place ablaze. The fire raged, consuming everything in its path. Josephus reports:

Roman soldiers carry items, including a menorah, looted from the temple before its destruction in 70 CE, in this frieze from the Arch of Titus in Rome. The arch was built in 81 CE to commemorate the emperor Titus's military successes.

Part of the skeleton of a woman uncovered in the "Burned House" in Jerusalem, a Jewish house that archaeological evidence indicates was set on fire and destroyed during the Roman siege of Jerusalem in 70 CE.

"Through the roar of the flames, streaming far and wide, the groans of the falling victims were heard . . . and the noise. Nothing more deafening or frightening could be imagined."

The temple fell on the ninth day of the Jewish month of Av. According to Jewish history, this was the same day Solomon's Temple had been razed by the Babylonians. Even today, Jews around the world remember the date with prayers and fasting.

After the temple fell, the Roman army continued its destruction of the city, smashing Herod's palace and other fine residences, as well as the homes and hovels of ordinary people. Blocks of stone littered the streets. Much of the Jewish population of Jerusalem was gone—either killed, escaped, or taken as slaves—but there remained pockets of fighting throughout Judaea. One band of Zealots made a futile last stand in the Judaean desert at a desolate fortress called Masada; it still stands today. Finally, in the year 73, the revolt was over.

Despite the devastation, Jerusalem was too large and populated a city to become completely uninhabited. For one thing, Rome used it as a base for its army. Non-Jews from other countries like Greece and Syria drifted in. Jewish followers of Jesus who had fled to Jordan at the start of the war slowly came back, and though their population had been decimated, some Jews remained.

Without the temple as a focus for their worship, Jews in Judaea and throughout the ancient world had to figure out a way to keep

The plateau and fortress of Masada, in the desert south of Jerusalem. A giant ramp used by the Roman army to attack the fortress is still visible on the left. Today it is a popular tourist site.

Judaism alive. They did this by concentrating on the words of the Torah, the first five books of the Bible. Torah study continued in places of learning called synagogues. Wherever Jews lived, synagogues were now the center of Jewish life.

In the year 130, the Roman emperor Hadrian arrived in Jerusalem and declared a huge rebuilding program that would raze what was left of the city, reinventing it as a new metropolis called Aelia Capitolina. Determined that the Jews, who were once again living there in substantial numbers, should bow to pressure and become conforming members of the empire, Hadrian issued laws against public gatherings and Jewish practices like teaching Torah. Especially appalling to the Jewish citizenry was Hadrian's idea of putting a temple to the Roman god Jupiter on the spot where the Jewish temple had once stood. This insult galvanized the people once more.

The final Jewish rebellion against Rome, in 132, was led by Simon Bar Kokhba, a seasoned soldier given the nickname Son of the Star by an influential rabbi. Bar Kokhba was thought by some to be the long-awaited Messiah. This must have encouraged people to fight on his side. Determined not to make the same mistakes made in other rebellions, Simon planned carefully and had success at first, wiping out Roman garrisons in the surrounding countryside and, after several years of fighting, getting a foothold in Jerusalem. But to think that he could outlast the Roman army, with its ever-increasing influx of new soldiers, was wishful thinking. In 135, the rebellion was put down, Bar Kokhba was killed, and the remaining Jews were expelled from Jerusalem.

The outcropping of rock that had been the center of the temple remained, but around it the new city of Aelia Capitolina was being built.

A mosaic map of Jerusalem shows the Roman layout of the city as it was constructed under the emperor Hadrian. A straight main street, the Cardo Maximus, begins at the northern gate and traverses the city. The map was created in the sixth century CE and is the oldest known map of Jerusalem.

7

FORGOTTEN

Aelia Capitolina flourished. Hadrian kept his promise to build a new, modern city with an amphitheater, city squares, and temples to the Roman gods.

The Roman soldiers who were stationed there continued to tear down what was left of the structures on the Mount, using the stone blocks for construction projects elsewhere in the city. Because the blocks used in the building of Temple Mount were distinctively carved, archaeologists have been able to easily locate them at other ancient Jerusalem sites. Despite the dismantling, the expanse of the Mount still stood.

Although Jews had been banished from the city, remnants of the Jewish population of Jerusalem continued to live throughout the region in places like Galilee and the nearby cities of Tiberias and Sepphoris. While Jews, nearby and farther away, may have dreamed of rebuilding the temple, they focused on the idea that Judaism was now centered in their synagogues and homes.

In the decades after the end of the Bar Kokhba rebellion in 135 CE, the Roman rulers came to see that the remaining Jews in

Judaea (which had also been renamed, as Palestinia) weren't going to pose any sort of threat. By the middle of the third century CE, they were allowed to come into Aelia Capitolina once a year, on the ninth day of Av in the Jewish calendar, the anniversary of the temple's two destructions, for one specific reason—to mourn the temple.

Those who came must have been filled with despair at the sight that met their eyes. Their holy city was now a pagan city, wiped clean of signs of the Jewish religion. Instead, there were temples and sites dedicated to Roman gods like Jupiter and Juno. A statue of Hadrian stood atop the Temple Mount.

An ancient document, found in the twentieth century, actually describes the scene: "These Jews would tear their clothes and weep for the temple and the people of Israel. Climbing to the desolate Temple Mount, they would offer prayers, and afterwards circle the gates of the city, as pilgrims often did in the old days. They still hoped that someday the Messiah would come and restore their city."

And what about the Christians? The centuries after Jesus's death were a time of turbulence and growth for what had begun as a small Jewish sect. As the Christian community began to expand and differentiate itself from the Jews, they faced their own persecutions from Rome. Like the Jews, early Christians were more devoted to their faith than to the idea of being part of the Roman Empire, which had civic duty and loyalty to the emperor at its core. The Christians were also more interested in the afterlife than the one here on earth, especially since that earthly life included worshipping the Roman emperor as a god, which went against everything they believed.

For some Christians the afterlife came early because of Roman persecution. Back in the year 64, Nero, an emperor known for his mental instability, was whispered to have started a massive fire in

Rome. Historians think it is unlikely that he did, but even so, he needed a scapegoat and blamed the fire on the Christians. That began a long period of government-sanctioned persecution in which Christians were crucified, beheaded, and even thrown to wild beasts— including lions and tigers—in Roman amphitheaters for the amusement of the crowd.

Although the deaths were horrific (and, today, some historians believe these deaths have been overestimated), members of the Christian community felt it was a badge of honor to die this way. Since Jesus had preached that the world would end soon, and believing a place in heaven awaited them, many of these men and women were willing martyrs (people who are executed for their faith).

A little more than three hundred years after the death of Jesus, in 306, a shrewd general named Constantine became one of the four rulers of the vast Roman Empire. His mother, Helena, was a Christian, so Constantine did not harbor the hatred of the religion that many officials of the empire did. In 312, according to Christian sources, in the midst of a decisive battle that would determine whether he would become the sole emperor, Constantine looked up in the sky and beheld an illuminated Christian symbol bearing the words, in Greek, "By this, win." He ordered his soldiers to put the symbol on their shields, and they triumphed in the Battle of Milvian Bridge.

The next year, 313, Constantine issued an edict that allowed Christians the freedom to follow their beliefs. Though Constantine did not outlaw other religions, he became a champion of Christianity. One of the most important things he did, at least as far as Jerusalem was concerned, was to send his mother there in 326 to find places and items important to Christianity.

And find things she did! Helena was said to have located both the

The entrance to the Church of the Nativity, built by Helena, mother of the Roman emperor Constantine, between 327 and 339 CE.

spot where Jesus was born and the spot where he died. Whether these were truly the exact places, it's hard to say. But with funds provided by her son, Helena built or refurbished the Church of the Nativity in Bethlehem and, near the Temple Mount, the Church of the Holy Sepulcher, which tradition said was the site of Jesus's crucifixion. With the help of local excavators, Helena even found what she believed were parts of the wooden cross on which Jesus died. She took them home with her and they can still be seen in Rome, although most scholars are doubtful the relics are authentic.

The continuous uprisings and war had kept away most believers in the decades after the temple's destruction in 70 CE. Then, after Jerusalem became Aelia Capitolina, there hadn't been much to see. But as the Roman Empire turned to Christianity, and thanks to Helena's identifying places associated with Jesus, the city began to be called Jerusalem once again and to attract numbers of religious pilgrims.

There had always been a trickle of people who wanted to spend time where Jesus had walked, preached, and died. The earliest evidence of these "tourists" comes, most archaeologists believe, from the second century. It is a picture scratched on a stone, thought to

A picture of a ship with the words "Lord, we came," scratched on a stone block discovered in the Church of the Holy Sepulcher in 1971.

be from Hadrian's time and discovered in the Church of the Holy Sepulcher. It clearly shows a drawing of a ship, and in Latin, the words "Lord, we came."

Another traveler, known as the Bordeaux pilgrim, coming from an area in today's France, left a record of his journey to Jerusalem in the mid-300s. There is a list of the holy sites he visited, including the Temple Mount. He mentions a specific rock that the Jewish mourners wail over on the ninth of Av. Is this the rock that has supposedly been in the same spot since Abraham's time? The one that had been revered since Solomon built the First Temple? The same rock pushing up through the floor of the Holy of Holies? It certainly seems to be.

Soon, more travelers were making their way to Jerusalem to worship and to wonder at Christian sites throughout the city. But even though Temple Mount was a place Jesus had visited several times, as recorded in the New Testament, it seems few people wanted to see it. Why not? For one thing, it remained abandoned and empty. Some observers wrote that it was now a garbage dump.

But the temple area also brought out harsh feelings among some Christians, especially those in charge of what was an increasingly powerful church. They looked at the destroyed, humbled ruins with satisfaction. According to Christian leaders, since most Jews had not accepted Jesus as the Messiah, the fate of their temple was deserved. In Christianity's eyes, faith in Jesus had replaced worship at the temple.

There was one brief moment when the Jewish people thought they might get their temple back. In 361, after the death of Constantine, a new emperor, Julian, came to the throne. He intensely disliked Christianity and was willing to allow the Jews to rebuild the temple. Work clearing the rubble from the temple site began almost immediately. Then, only a few months later, Julian was killed in battle. The next emperor turned back to Christianity. Plans for a new temple died in the dirt.

For more than three hundred years, the city of Jerusalem flourished, but the temple site remained abandoned and desolate. Then, in 638, a wind came out of the desert. Islam arrived in the Holy Land, and the Temple Mount came alive once more.

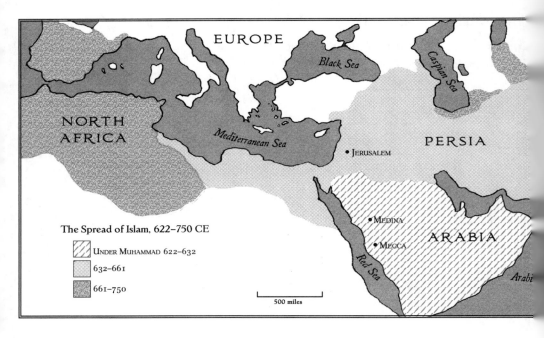

The Spread of Islam, 622–750 CE

EUROPE

Black Sea

Caspian Sea

NORTH
AFRICA

Mediterranean Sea

• JERUSALEM

PERSIA

• MEDINA

• MECCA

ARABIA

Red Sea

Arabi

UNDER MUHAMMAD 622–632

632–661

661–750

500 miles

THE NOBLE SANCTUARY

In a rocky cave, eight hundred miles or so from Jerusalem, a man named Muhammad meditated.

Muhammad was known as one of the most upright and honest men in the prosperous Arabian city of Mecca. A merchant by trade, he would regularly travel several miles from the city to a cave at Mount Hira to be with his thoughts, to fast, and to contemplate. The Arab population of Mecca and the surrounding areas believed in a range of gods. But Muhammad, very much like Abraham, was convinced that there was only one God, Allah, the Arabic name for the supreme God. And Muhammad believed Allah was the same true God worshipped by the Jews and Christians he had met during his many years in commerce.

In the year 610, during Ramadan, the ninth month in the Arabic calendar, forty-year-old Muhammad was meditating when he had a terrifying experience. As a writer today describes it, "An invisible presence crushed him in its embrace . . . He was overwhelmed by darkness." He heard a voice command him, "Recite!" But he did not know what to say. The presence tightened its grip. Only when he thought he could stand no more did he receive direction from the presence, who, according to Islamic tradition, was the angel Gabriel: "Recite in the name of your Lord who created, / Created humanity from a clot of blood." God, Gabriel continued, was going to reveal to Muhammad lessons He wanted people to learn.

So begins the religion of Islam, a word that means "submission." It asks people to surrender to the will of Allah. At first, a shaken Muhammad did not discuss this overwhelming event and later ones like it except with his wife and closest friends. But Muhammad did recite the verses that came to him, which he understood to be the words of God. They told how men and women should live in harmony, take care of the poor, and turn away from idols and only worship Allah.

By 613, Muhammad began to share these insights with others. He wanted people to know that there was one God, Allah, and that Allah's concern was that there be an equal society. But this news had no appeal for most of the citizens of Mecca, loyal only to their own tribes and their pantheon of gods, and determined to keep their wealth. Muhammad was ridiculed and even threatened, especially by the Quraysh, Mecca's most powerful tribe. After years of teaching, he had only a small group of followers, a number of them on the margins of society, including women and the poor.

However, there were people interested in Muhammad's message. Representatives from the city of Yathrib (now called Medina), about 250 miles away, had heard that Muhammad was a wise and upright man. Their city was in turmoil, with tribes fighting one another, so they invited him to come with his followers and settle their disputes. Muhammad arrived in Medina around 622, and he quickly gained stature among its citizens.

Some of the Arab population of Medina followed the Jewish

religion. (The term "Arab" refers to an ethnicity. People who share an ethnicity identify with one another because they have the same heritage and culture. Judaism, Christianity, and Islam are religions.) While in Medina, Muhammad learned that the Jews believed the Arab people were descended from Abraham through his son Ishmael. This confirmed what Muhammad already believed: Allah was the God of Abraham, the God worshipped by Jews and Christians.

Muhammad thought Jews, and later Christians, would join him in Islam. Most did not. But the Arab tribes in the region became more receptive to Muhammad's message and they began joining the Islamic community. Islam began to spread quickly through the Arabian Peninsula. By 630, Muhammad had returned to Mecca in triumph, and the gates of the city were opened to him.

From that first overwhelming moment when he felt touched by Allah in the Hira cave, and for the next twenty-three years until his death in 632, Muhammad continued to receive revelations. These verses were compiled into a book, the Quran, which means "the Recitation." The words of the Quran, which Muslims regard as the word of God, confirm that Muhammad was God's prophet. And while Islam acknowledges and reveres earlier prophets—Abraham, Moses, and Jesus among them—it views Muhammad as the final prophet.

The cities of Mecca, where Muhammad was born, and Medina, where he is buried, both now in Saudi Arabia, are the holiest cities in Islam. But Islam also has a third holy place, and that is Jerusalem.

Jerusalem's importance to Islam comes from a short mention in the Quran and a more detailed report in other Islamic writings called the Hadith, a collection of oral accounts of Muhammad's life. This particular story has come to be known as "The Night Journey." Jerusalem is not mentioned by name, but according to the story Muhammad

HARAM AL-SHARIF
The Noble Sanctuary
c. 700 CE

Al-Aqsa Mosque

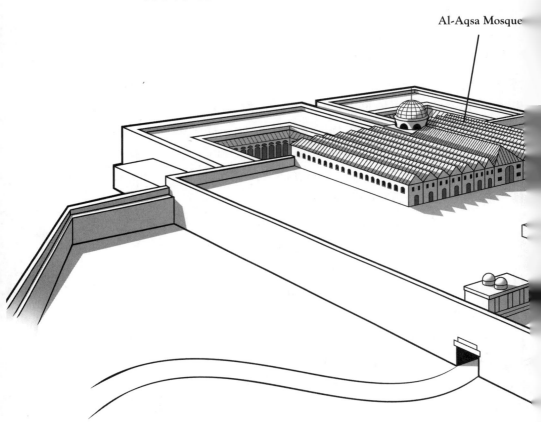

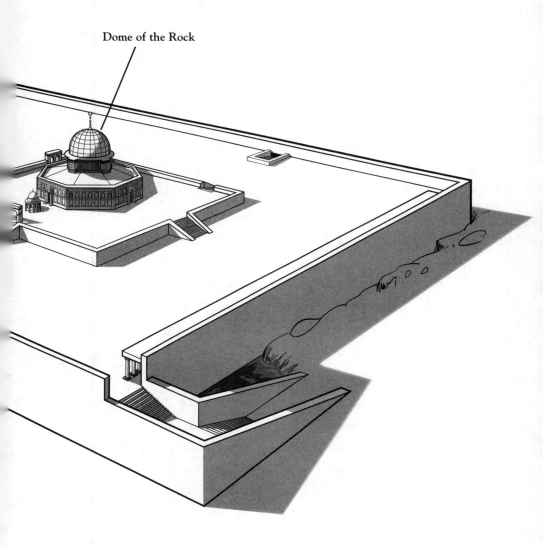

Dome of the Rock

mounts a winged white steed called Buraq that takes him from "the Sacred Mosque" in Mecca to "the farthest Mosque," which in Islamic tradition is the Temple Mount in Jerusalem.

And here is where our rock returns to the story. At the Temple Mount, Muhammad leads a group of prophets in prayer. Then, accompanied by the angel Gabriel, he ascends into heaven, where he again sees the prophets—Adam, Abraham, and Moses among them. He meets, too, with Allah, and is given some important rules for his followers, including the obligation that Muslims should pray five times a day.

A small indentation in the rock, which can still be seen, is said by some to be either Muhammad's footprint, made when he ascended, or the mark of Buraq's hoof; others believe it is the handprint of Gabriel, made as the angel held back the rock to prevent it from following Muhammad to heaven.

Muhammad died in 632. The rise and success of Islam was sure and swift. The Arabian Peninsula (most of which is today taken up by Saudi Arabia) was the cradle of Islam. Through persuasion and sometimes force, masses of people converted, and soon Islam was sweeping across the Middle East. Only five years after Muhammad's death, Muslim forces were ready to strike Jerusalem.

In 637, Jerusalem was a Christian city. Religious pilgrims flocked there; the places that were important to the lives of Jesus and his early followers were everywhere one turned, and many of those places were marked by churches. Jews had again been banned from Jerusalem, though a scattered few remained. The once Jewish city was now the spiritual center of the Christian world.

Despite observing the success of Muslim troops elsewhere, the people of Jerusalem were not well prepared for battle. There was a terrible sense of dread for Christians when Islamic armies appeared at the gates, armed and ready to take the city. The leader in charge of Jerusalem, a church leader named Sophronius, rallied what troops he had on hand and tried to mount a defense, but after seven months that effort failed. In 638, Jerusalem surrendered.

The man they surrendered to, Umar I, was the second caliph, or successor, to Muhammad. At first a persecutor of Muhammad, he had become one of his strongest supporters and a successful general. Umar tried to live his life simply, as the Prophet had, even wearing an old patched tunic and carrying his own military gear.

Accounts of the surrender say that Umar came into the city riding a white camel. Believing deeply, as Muhammad did, that Allah was the same God worshipped by Jews and Christians, he had no desire to murder or destroy those who also believed in the one true deity. So for one of the few times in a thousand years, a triumphant power came into Jerusalem after a siege unaccompanied by killing or burning or destruction; there was no looting of property, no expulsion of citizens. Christians and the Jews who still lived there were not required to convert to Islam.

This peaceful entry allowed Sophronius to take Umar on a tour of Jerusalem. One stop on this tour shocked the Muslim general: his first sight of the Temple Mount area. It had been used as the town dump. Filthy and stinking, it was filled with garbage that rose almost to the top of the structure's remaining archways. Umar insisted on climbing on his hands and knees through the muck up to the platform that once held the temple. What greeted him was an expanse of rubble and desolation. Umar vowed that this desecration of such a holy site would not stand.

Umar asked some of the remaining Jews and Jewish converts to

Islam to identify where the Temple itself had once stood on the Mount as the cleanup began. Eventually, seventy Jewish families were allowed back into Jerusalem. The Jewish population thought Islam was closer to Jewish beliefs than Christianity was, and came to prefer Muslim rule. Some even harbored the hope that perhaps the temple might be rebuilt.

But make no mistake, the temple was not going to be rebuilt. Umar and his soldiers and others who accompanied him into Jerusalem needed a mosque for prayer. One of the first things Muhammad had done when he came to Medina was construct a place of worship that also served as a meeting place for his family and companions. Now Umar did the same. A simple oblong wooden structure was erected on the Mount. It was so plain that a Christian pilgrim who saw it in about 670 described it dismissively as "a four-sided house of prayer, which they have built rudely, constructing boards and great beams on the remains of ruins." Still, it could hold thousands of people. Later, in 705, a larger building replaced the first mosque. Today, a rebuilt, enlarged, and more ornamental mosque stands in the same place. It is known as the Al-Aqsa Mosque.

Nearby, the Dome of the Rock was commissioned by a later caliph, Abd al-Malik, in 688, fifty years after Umar's entrance into Jerusalem. The Muslim community in Jerusalem, though it lived calmly with Jews and Christians, was surrounded by impressive Christian buildings, particularly the Church of the Holy Sepulcher, which covered its own important historical rock: the burial tomb of Jesus. A tenth-century Islamic historian noted that the Muslims, too, "wanted monuments that were unique and a wonder to the world."

The Dome of the Rock is not a mosque. It is a shrine to honor the rock. And a rock embracing such history and legend, absorbing so many dreams and hopes, once again needed a proper home, one that spoke of its significance and importance. A home that would recall the glory of the only God to all those who saw it.

Although we do not know how the Muslims knew exactly where the rock was located, it is likely that the Jews and Jewish converts to Islam who had assisted in the first clearing of the Temple Mount had some idea of where the Holy of Holies once stood. As more Jews returned to Jerusalem, further information about the rock's location probably became available.

The rock, also known as the Foundation Stone, enclosed within the Dome of the Rock atop the Noble Sanctuary.

The Dome of the Rock today.

By 692, the Dome of the Rock was completed. From the center of the Temple Mount, now known by its Muslim name, Haram al-Sharif, the Noble Sanctuary, rose a magnificent eight-sided structure. It has been called "the most beautiful and perfect achievement of Islamic architecture." The Dome of the Rock has become more impressive decoratively as the centuries have gone on, but its basic structure has remained the same. The lower outside walls, made of lustrous marble, met walls of colored glass mosaics in intricate geometric designs. The brilliant dome itself, more than sixty-five feet in diameter, was constructed from a double-shell design, made of wood, and originally covered with gold from melted coins.

The inside of the shrine was equally beautiful. The walls featured polished marble, golden mosaics, and burnished woodwork. A series of arches enclosed the huge, pockmarked rock, the building's focus. Islam does not depict living beings in religious art. But there is no law forbidding bringing representations of nature inside; the interior of the building was covered with mosaics of flowers and plants. The interior of the dome itself was intricately designed with elaborate red and gold floral motifs. Stained-glass windows circled the interior, as did verses from the Quran, written in flowing script.

But the Dome of the Rock was more to Muslims than just a stunning building. As one contemporary author put it: "Its exterior, which reaches toward the infinity of the sky, is a perfect replica of its internal dimension. It illustrates the way the divine and the human, the inner and outer worlds fit and complement one another as two halves of a single whole." It is a spiritual center. It is a place "where heaven and earth met."

With the completion of the Dome of the Rock, the Islamic presence in Jerusalem was now established and sanctified by the shrine and the mosque. The three religions of Abraham now lived in Jerusalem, sometimes without incident, sometimes under stress, but for the next four hundred years under Islamic rule.

However, Christians outside the Holy Land had not forgotten that the city was once theirs. And the time was coming when they would want it back.

9

9

THE TEMPLE MOUNT RETAKEN

G od wills it!"

That was what Pope Urban II told the Council of Clermont, a gathering of hundreds of bishops and noblemen from France and Italy, in 1095. God, he said, wanted the faithful from all classes of medieval life—knights, tradespeople, priests, peasants—to go to Jerusalem and take back the holy city from the Muslims.

"God wills it!" the crowd roared back.

It was Pope Urban's fiery speech that began the first Crusade. *Crusade* comes from a French word that means "to take up the cross." When the leader of the eastern Christian Empire in Constantinople asked the pope in Rome for troops to help him fight the Muslim Turks who had taken over most of his territory, he expected perhaps a garrison or two. But Pope Urban had a much bigger idea. He wanted Jerusalem back in Christian hands.

It's hard to imagine in this day of the Internet, texts, and social media how news could travel quickly in an era when the only means of communication was letter writing or word of mouth. Yet the call for a Crusade, proclaimed in churches across Europe, was heard by thousands of men, women, and even children, who would soon head toward Jerusalem as soldiers for Christ.

Those who answered the call did so for all sorts of reasons. Jerusalem and its sacred spaces were a part of the popular imagination in the Middle Ages, appearing in stories, art, and ballads. So many felt it was an abomination that Christian holy places were in the hands of Muslims. But others were lured to join the Crusade by the idea of wealth or adventure, including poor people who didn't have much to lose. And there was one more important incentive: the pope promised that everyone who took up the cross would be absolved of all their sins.

Most participants, even those with motives of profit in mind, still thought they were doing God's will. But it is hard to imagine that God wanted the bloody massacre that would come with the Crusaders' arrival in Jerusalem.

In the four hundred years since the Muslims had taken over Jerusalem, there had been periods of both stability and instability in the city. For one thing, there were arguments in the larger Muslim world about Muhammad's successors, which led to Islam splitting into two groups, the Shia and the Sunni. The Shia wanted the successors to come from Muhammad's family; the Sunni disagreed with this line of thought. Still, Islam continued to grow. By the year 1000, it is estimated there were ten million Muslims living in a wide swath from Gibraltar off the coast of Spain to the Himalayas in Asia. The Middle East was predominantly Muslim.

Closer to home, there was territorial fighting between different Muslim tribes, ethnic groups, and small kingdoms in the areas surrounding Jerusalem. All were vying for the money and prestige that came with being in charge of the holy city, and power regularly changed hands, often after heated battles.

As rulers changed and Islam's power grew, so did opinions about how the other citizens of Jerusalem—the Christians and Jews—should be treated. Commonalities became less important. Most Muslims now wanted Islam to be recognized as the superior religion.

Though they were often treated as second-class citizens, Christians and Jews were still able to worship at their holy sites (a synagogue had even been built near the Mount area), but they were taxed more heavily than Muslims and had fewer rights. Jerusalem also saw in-fighting among Jews, and various groups of Christians squabbled with one another, too.

Sometimes it seemed as if the land itself was finding it difficult to withstand all the deadly arguments. A series of earthquakes, especially a severe one in 1033, jolted the city, damaging some religious sites, including the Dome of the Rock, which had to be renovated. Still, despite the danger and the hardships, pilgrims of all three religions continued to make their way to Jerusalem, and the money they spent was a great boon to the city.

The first Crusade officially began in the summer of 1096, when an army of about 40,000 soldiers along with a stream of peasants and clergy set off through eastern Europe. The pope had originally insisted women not go, but they went anyway. In the fall, tens of thousands more people followed. The journey was arduous. Illness and hunger struck and bloody battles were fought along the way. Many people died. It was a starving, decimated group of Crusaders that ultimately made its way to Jerusalem in the summer of 1099.

Yet, as weakened as the Crusaders were when Jerusalem came

into sight, hardened soldiers screamed and yelled almost in disbelief. Some wept. Others fell to their knees and prayed.

The Crusaders came prepared to fight. They immediately put catapults in place to throw rocks and other projectiles over Jerusalem's fortified walls. Most of the Christians living in Jerusalem had fled or been thrown out of the city: the Muslim leaders were well aware that an assault was in the making and they didn't want Christians helping the enemy. But some of those Christians made their way to the Crusaders, and their knowledge of the city helped the Crusaders prepare for the siege.

After a few weeks of preparation, on July 15, 1099, the Crusaders stormed Jerusalem. During three days of fighting, the Crusaders killed

Medieval European manuscript illustration showing the siege of Jerusalem in 1099.

nearly everyone they found—men, women, and children. The battle ended at the Noble Sanctuary. The Muslims made one last stand on the roof of the Al-Aqsa Mosque, to no avail. They were all killed. Jews who had taken refuge in their nearby synagogue were slaughtered when the Crusaders burned the building. It is estimated 30,000 people died in the siege of Jerusalem.

After the carnage was over, the Crusaders tried to get the city running again. The first thing they did was attempt to burn the dead bodies to stave off disease, though by some accounts they weren't entirely successful, with body parts visible months later. Another problem was that few of the fighters wanted to stay in Jerusalem. Most of the Crusaders felt that with the city in Christian hands, their job was done. They were ready to gather their plunder, including the riches they had taken from the dead, and go home.

The new leader of Jerusalem was a knight named Godfrey of Bouillon. He immediately moved his headquarters into the Al-Aqsa Mosque on the Temple Mount (Christians would no longer call it the Noble Sanctuary). The Dome of the Rock was converted into a church, now called the Temple of the Lord.

In July 1100, less than a year after the Crusaders' victory, Godfrey died of typhoid fever and was succeeded by his brother Baldwin, who had several goals. He wanted to make allies of the local Christians, who were mostly Arabs and had more in common with Muslim Arabs than they did with European Christians, and he wanted to encourage more Christians to live in Jerusalem. He was successful on both counts. Some of the local Arab Christians moved to the city. And Baldwin's proclamation that anyone who lived in the city for a year and a day was entitled to a house and land helped the population grow back into the thousands.

A royal seal from the period of Crusader rule of Jerusalem shows the Dome of the Rock with a cross atop its dome.

Baldwin was also eager to make sure that the Dome of the Rock would remain explicitly identified as a Christian building. In 1115, it was refurbished inside and out. A huge cross was erected on the top of the dome. Inside, the verses of the Quran, some of which insisted that God would not and did not have a son, were covered over.

Security around Jerusalem was a problem that was more difficult to solve. The now Christian city was surrounded by Muslim towns and enclaves. Religious pilgrims, still the biggest source of Jerusalem's income, were being robbed and murdered along their way to visit the holy sites. So it was a great relief to Baldwin when, in 1118, a group of knights came to him with an offer. They would protect the pilgrims as they journeyed through enemy lands. They called themselves the Poor Knights of Christ, but when Baldwin gave them headquarters on the Temple Mount, they became known as the Knights of the Temple of Solomon, or the Knights Templar.

If that name sounds familiar, it's because all sorts of legends and stories have grown up around these knights in the almost 1,000 years since they approached Baldwin. The Knights Templar have been a part of many books, have had prominent roles in movies, and have even been featured in video games. Almost from the time the Templars organized

Crosses scratched on the wall of the Church of the Holy Sepulcher by pilgrims and Crusader soldiers.

themselves, there has been speculation about hidden artifacts they might have found on the Temple Mount where they were stationed.

The most often-told tale about the Knights Templar is that they came into possession of the Holy Grail, the cup that Jesus used at the Last Supper—a cup that has accumulated more and more magical properties as the centuries have passed. Another says the knights found the Ark of the Covenant. While these stories are the stuff legends are made of, it is true that the knights acquired relics and wealth. As their fame and power grew, they received donations from throughout Europe and their treasury served as a bank for the pilgrims they were protecting, which made them money as well. The Knights Templar may have started out as the Poor Knights of Christ, but in time they became very powerful and very, very rich.

The Knights Templar took a deep interest in the Temple Mount, where they had their headquarters, but mostly with an eye to turning it into a military stronghold. The old Al-Aqsa Mosque was once again enlarged and a new wing was added. The building now housed weapons and grain, and featured lavatories. One monk reported seeing gardens on the roof. The knights kept their horses—thousands of them—under the Mount itself, in the vaulted area they called Solomon's Stables.

As the Crusaders became at home in Jerusalem—even taking up such local customs as bathing, an activity practically ignored in Europe—the architecture of the city soon began to take on the style of the victor. Not only were the Muslim buildings converted into churches, older churches were refurbished, and new shrines throughout the city marked places where Jesus and his followers had walked and preached. Pilgrims were treated to detailed tours, including of the Temple Mount, which was now considered an important Christian religious site, with the focus on stories—not all of them true—about events in the life of Jesus that had taken place there. Islamic legends became Christian tales: Muhammad's footprint on the rock was now shown to pilgrims as Jesus's handprint.

Solomon's Stables, a vaulted area beneath the Temple Mount used by Christian soldiers to stable their horses, in a photograph taken before the area was refurbished as a mosque in 1996.

The Jerusalem Citadel—originally Herod's palace, and subsequently both a Christian and a Muslim fortress, depending on who governed the city.

10

SALADIN AND SULEIMAN

As time went on, the city leaders, the Knights Templar, and other religious and military groups took steps to ensure Jerusalem's safety by fortifying the city. There were, however, things that couldn't be changed. Jerusalem remained a rather small Christian city in the middle of a huge swath of Muslim territory.

In the years between 1169 and 1174, a charismatic Muslim leader named Saladin came to power in Egypt. He conquered and united his territories with those of Syria and other kingdoms and went on to fight Crusader armies around Jerusalem, culminating in the Battle of Hattin in July 1187, where the Christian forces were roundly defeated. Now, Saladin and his army were ready to take back Jerusalem.

Prepared to avenge the massacre of 1099, Saladin sent a message to the city's Christian leaders: "We shall deal with you just as you dealt with the population when you took Jerusalem, with murder and enslavement and other such savageries."

Then something unusual happened. Baron Balian, the leader of the Christians inside Jerusalem's walls, sent a message to Saladin.

Balian argued that though outnumbered, Christians would still kill as many Muslim soldiers as possible and destroy the shrines and buildings on the Mount so they wouldn't fall into enemy hands. Why not let the Christians surrender and avoid destruction and bloodshed?

To the surprise of many on both sides, Saladin agreed. On October 2, 1187, less than a hundred years after the Crusaders had taken over, Saladin and his army marched peacefully into Jerusalem. It was a Muslim city once more.

What did that mean? The crosses on buildings came down. Churches were converted to mosques. The Noble Sanctuary was purified, and any trace of Christianity on the Temple Mount (including that name) disappeared. These kinds of changes were expected when the city changed hands. There were a few differences, however, in how Saladin ruled.

For one thing, Saladin allowed Jews to return to Jerusalem. In 1190, a synagogue was built, which brought more Jews from the surrounding area and from farther afield. Saladin died in 1193, but his practice of letting Jews return to the city continued after his death.

Saladin also let Christians keep control of some of their religious places, like the Church of the Holy Sepulcher. He even permitted Christian soldiers to stay in the area, giving them a slice of land outside Jerusalem.

This decision was a rare misstep for Saladin: the presence of a Christian army near Jerusalem gave hope to European Christians that they could retake the city. Several more Crusades were launched in the twelfth and thirteenth centuries. (From 1096 to 1291 there were seven major Crusades and many lesser ones.)

These later Crusades were not successful, but around the year 1218, the ruler of Jerusalem, Sultan al-Mu'azzam Isa (who lived in Damascus), decided it might be best to simply stop defending the city. In 1220, the sultan's army was sent to tear down Jerusalem's defensive walls. Other leaders of Jerusalem were horrified, as were the terrified citizens, and with Christian soldiers on the march, much of the population left the city.

In any event, this group of Crusaders returned home before they ever got to Jerusalem. But during the launch of yet another Crusade, in 1229, another sultan, Al-Malik al-Kamil, also did not want to fight the Crusaders. The Crusade's leader, Holy Roman Emperor Frederick II, didn't want the fight either; he was involved in a dispute with the pope and had only a weak army under his command. Frederick, who had an affinity for Islam, proposed a treaty that would return Jerusalem to the Crusaders, but leave the Noble Sanctuary under Muslim control and prohibit fortification of the city.

Al-Kamil agreed and a treaty to last for ten years was signed in 1229. Despite the peace it brought, ordinary citizens of both faiths were outraged by the compromise. Al-Kamil was hated as a traitor, even though Jerusalem's Muslim sites were left in Islamic hands. The Christians, too, were furious. How dare an emperor who had the word *holy* in his title allow Muslims to stay in Jerusalem without a fight? When Frederick visited Jerusalem, he was almost assassinated. The treaty expired in 1239, and after a period of skirmishes, Jerusalem went back to Muslim hands.

The city remained in relative calm for several hundred years and even prospered under a dynasty called the Mamluk, but eventually regimes grew weaker, the economy faltered, Bedouin raiders became bolder, and Jerusalem was once more poor and unsafe.

Then a powerful new leader came to Jerusalem.

Suleiman (the Arabic form of the name Solomon) was known as "the Magnificent." A brilliant general and a learned scholar, he was born in Turkey and presided over the Ottoman Empire from 1520 until his death in 1566. The Ottoman Empire was a huge amount of territory that by the end of his reign contained much of North Africa, western Asia, the Middle East, and parts of southern Europe. Dynamic and full of ideas, Suleiman wanted to bring Jerusalem, which had become part of the Ottoman Empire in 1517, back to its former glory.

To that end, he began an ambitious building program. Beginning around 1535, he rebuilt the walls of the city and began a beautification project that included lush gardens and bubbling fountains. Naturally, the beautification extended to the Noble Sanctuary. The

The Damascus Gate, part of the monumental city walls built by Suleiman the Magnificent in the sixteenth century CE, in a nineteenth-century photograph.

Dome of the Rock, which had been restored under Saladin, became even more glorious, with marble added to the inside, richly colored tiles to the outside, and more gilt applied to the dome.

But Suleiman was also committed to having a safer, more inclusive Jerusalem. He subdued the Bedouin tribes that had been endangering pilgrims and tourists, and he made the city more open to those of all faiths who wanted to visit its sacred spaces.

Once again, the Jewish people, whose presence in the city had been discouraged, were allowed back to Jerusalem. With the Temple Mount now fully transformed into the Noble Sanctuary, any hope of turning it back into a Jewish place of worship was long gone. The Jews, however, had found a spot that seemed to them the place where their holy spirit now rested: the Western Wall.

Although Herod's Temple had been destroyed almost 1,500 years earlier by the Romans, this segment of one of the original stone walls that had held up the platform had, over the centuries, become a place where Jews gathered to be close to God. Archaeology has taught us that this Western Wall (in more recent times sometimes called the Wailing Wall—primarily by non-Jews—because of the emotion it elicits from Jewish visitors) was not a holy site in the days of Herod's Temple. Most historians think that small shops were set up against the wall, like one of today's outdoor markets, so it was a place of commerce in Herod's time, not of prayer.

But it's unlikely that the Jews who came to visit the wall in Suleiman's time knew all that. What they did know was that this was a structure linked to their temple. By the twelfth and thirteenth centuries, religious tourists were already writing about the Western Wall and how it was a site of Jewish prayer. As Suleiman allowed more

The Western Wall, in a nineteenth-century photograph.

Jews into Jerusalem, many settled near the wall in what would come to be called the Jewish Quarter.

In 1566, Suleiman died. At the time of his death, the Ottoman Empire was one of the world's strongest powers. All the important Muslim cities—Mecca, Medina, Cairo, Baghdad, and, of course,

Jerusalem—were united in the empire. The empire continued for hundreds of years.

In Jerusalem, those years were filled with what had become normal: disagreements and fighting among the various religious groups that lived there. Different sects of Christians argued with one another over who should be in charge of their holy places. Jews from the Middle East squabbled with an influx of Jewish settlers from Europe. And as time went on, no one, not even the Muslim citizens, liked the city rulers put in place by the Ottoman Empire, which grew more corrupt.

This corruption took its toll, and the Ottoman Empire weakened. As the twentieth century approached, things were about to change in Jerusalem once more. Probably no one—Muslims, Christians, or Jews—had any idea how dramatic that change would be.

Jerusalem in the 1860s.

11

TWO PEOPLES, TWO HOMELANDS

There have always been Jews in and around Jerusalem. Whenever they were thrown out, a number of them stayed nearby. Whenever the gates of the city were opened to them again—most notably by Muslim leaders like Suleiman—they returned.

But by the middle of the 1800s, most Jews lived in other places: Germany, Russia, Poland, and throughout the Middle East in the cities of the Ottoman Empire. A community of Jews could be found almost anywhere on earth.

In 1840, there were about 11,000 people in Jerusalem: about 4,500 Muslims; 3,500 Christians; and 3,000 Jews. Just before the American Civil War, in 1860, the population of Jerusalem was about 18,000 people: 6,000 Muslims; 4,000 Christians; and 8,000 Jews. By 1885, there were 15,000 Jews in Jerusalem.

There were many reasons Jews were coming back to Jerusalem, but number one was how little safety they had in Europe. At the time of the first Crusade, in the eleventh century, Jews had been killed by Christians on their way to Jerusalem who believed the Jewish people were responsible for the death of Jesus. Over the centuries, when things went wrong, anything from a financial crisis to an outbreak of illness, Jews were often blamed. Jewish communities in both Europe and the Middle East in the 1500s, 1600s, and 1700s were constantly in danger of being persecuted and dislodged.

In Spain, for instance, Jews were once a prosperous part of the community. But in 1492, King Ferdinand II and Queen Isabella, the same rulers who championed the explorer Christopher Columbus, decreed that all Jews were to be expelled from the country. Hundreds of thousands fled and found homes in Italy, Turkey, and even South America.

In the 1860s, a Jew living in Germany, Moses Hess, felt the rumblings of anti-Semitism—prejudice against the Jewish people—starting to build in his country. He and others began discussing a solution: a Jewish homeland. Not all of them thought it had to be in their ancient land, but most involved in the homeland movement did want it in the place that was linked to the Jews through history and religion. When a groom at a Jewish wedding stomped on a glass, it was to remind everyone of the destruction of the temple. At the end of every Passover seder, the dinner guests would raise their glasses and say, "Next year in Jerusalem." If there was to be a country for the Jews, a place of safety that they could not be forced to leave, the natural site, it seemed to many, was their historic home, Israel.

Of course, there was no "Israel" at this time. Jerusalem and the surrounding areas were now all part of the decaying Ottoman Empire. But that didn't stop a growing number of primarily European Jews from dreaming that someday a country called Israel would exist.

Jewish communities around the world continued to experience prejudice. During the late nineteenth century, things were

Jews being assaulted during a violent riot, or pogrom, in Kiev, Ukraine, in the 1880s.

particularly bad for Jewish communities in Russia. Isolated and heavily taxed, the Jews endured a series of pogroms, or organized massacres, that left their towns destroyed and the people sometimes killed and always terrorized. A mass exodus from Russia began. A majority of those Jews went to the United States, a land, they felt, of unlimited opportunity. But a number of Jews chose to go to Jerusalem and the surrounding area, which was now called Palestine.

Many of those settlers were not in the least religious. They didn't really care that the Temple Mount had been turned into the Noble Sanctuary. What they cared about was the land. These settlers were socialists—they believed both work and reward should be divided among men and women living in collectives, or, in Hebrew, kibbut-zim. It wasn't easy for Europeans to get used to working in the hot desert climate, and some left, but they were replaced by even more settlers.

Settlers from Russia working at a kibbutz in Palestine, 1912.

Even if they didn't care about following traditional Jewish law or customs, these settlers still thought of themselves as Jews. Their movement was called Zionism, from the ancient name of Mount Zion. Coming back to the land was called, in Hebrew, *aliya*, which means "going up" or "ascent." Just as Jewish worshippers at the ancient temple site made their way ever up toward God, Jewish settlers believed their *aliya* was to leave their old, troubled lives behind and move up to a better place.

How did the Muslim population in Jerusalem view this settlers' movement? With alarm. After all, Jerusalem was a city they had controlled since 1187. Its holiest site, the Noble Sanctuary, had been managed in one form or another since that date by an entity called the Waqf. Loosely defined, this is a Muslim religious or charitable foundation. Even today, though the Noble Sanctuary is in the Jewish state of Israel, this trust continues to be in charge of affairs that include the Al-Aqsa Mosque and the Dome of the Rock. Not all the

Arabs living in Palestine were Muslim. Some were Christian, and they, too, looked at Zionism with deep suspicion.

In 1917, during World War I, the British defeated what was left of the Ottoman Empire and took Palestine under its protection. Great Britain had, for a number of years, been a strong supporter of a Jewish homeland. There were several reasons for this. Biblical archaeology had begun in earnest in the mid-1860s, and many discoveries of both artifacts and manuscripts had captured the British imagination. Discoveries going back to biblical times fed into a belief among British Christians that, according to their reading of the Bible, Jesus would not return to earth for the Second Coming until the Jews were regathered in Israel.

More pragmatically, the British did not want France to gain a stronghold in Palestine. And on a personal level, men like Theodor Herzl, a leading advocate of Zionism in the late 1800s, gathered support from influential world citizens. Several decades later, a persuasive Russian Jew named Chaim Weizmann convinced important British politicians like Winston Churchill to support the movement's ideas.

In 1917, after the British were established in Palestine, they issued the Balfour Declaration: "His Majesty's government views with favour the establishment in Palestine of a national home for the Jewish people . . . it being clearly understood that nothing shall be done which may prejudice the civil and religious rights of existing non-Jewish communities in Palestine."

The declaration, which was more a letter of intent than of action, acknowledged the rights of Muslim citizens (and of Christians), but understandably, this act was seen by those groups as a betrayal by the British. Tensions between the Jewish and Muslim communities grew, often resulting in armed fights and more killings, sometimes right at the foot of the Western Wall. In time both sides turned against the British and the way they were managing Palestine.

In 1933, Adolf Hitler and his Nazi Party came to power in Germany. The Nazis despised their Jewish citizens and blamed many of their social and financial ills on them. They began the destruction of Jewish communities. In fact, the Nazis had a "final solution" for the "problem" of Jews in Germany and throughout Europe: they would kill them all. As the Germans marched into Poland, France, the Netherlands, and other countries of Europe, they also formed plans to round up the Jews of each nation and place them in concentration camps to be exterminated. As World War II raged, the Nazi regime not only fought the Allies—which included Russia, the United States, and Great Britain and its Commonwealth countries—but also systematically murdered millions of Jews, as well as other people they found "undesirable": homosexuals, the mentally and physically impaired, and the Romany people, known then as Gypsies.

Today, this chain of mass killings is known as the Holocaust. But at the time there was no clear understanding of what was happening. Some people knew. Many, many more suspected. The Nazis had made their intentions known, but there was disbelief and sometimes willful ignorance about the breadth and scope of their plans. In any case, the Allies' focus was on winning the war. It was not until World War II was over and the concentration camps were liberated that the full horror of the Holocaust was on display for the world to see. Six million Jews, adults and children, had been killed. Millions of others had had their lives destroyed. Sympathy turned to the Jews. Support for a Jewish homeland grew.

The problem, from the Arab perspective, was that there were already people who had a homeland in Palestine—them. They, like

Explosions in the Old City of Jerusalem during the 1948 war.

others, might have sympathy for what the Jews had gone through, but why should they have to suffer for what had happened in Europe? The idea of dividing their home, Palestine, was met with anger and anguish.

The brand-new United Nations, formed after World War II, grappled with the problem. On November 29, 1947, it decided to partition Palestine, creating two states—in its words, one Arab, one Jewish—with Jerusalem becoming an international city that would be open to Muslims, Christians, and Jews.

This was not acceptable to the Arab population, which would lose territory in a plan they felt was being forced on them. War raged

A family of Palestinian refugees at the so-called "Green Line" separating Arab- and Jewish-held territory after the end of the 1948 war.

between the Jews and the Arabs of Palestine, but by the spring of 1948, the Jewish side was in command. On May 15, 1948, Israel declared itself a state. Palestinians remember this as Nakba, the Day of Catastrophe. Each year it commemorates the people displaced by the new state. In response to the declaration, four Arab countries— Egypt, Syria, Jordan, and Iraq—declared war on Israel.

A year later, both sides agreed to a cease-fire. There would be no Palestinian state coexisting alongside Israel; instead, Jordan took control of the western part of the territory, as well as East Jerusalem, which included the Old City, where the Noble Sanctuary, the Church of the Holy Sepulcher, and many other important religious sites of Islam, Christianity, and Judaism were located. After the division, Jews were barred from praying at the Western Wall.

ISRAELI–HELD TERRITORY
BEFORE AND AFTER THE SIX-DAY WAR OF 1967

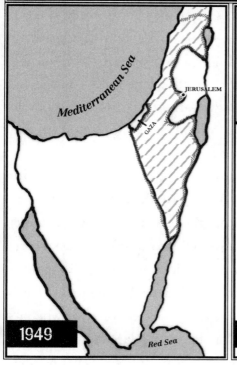

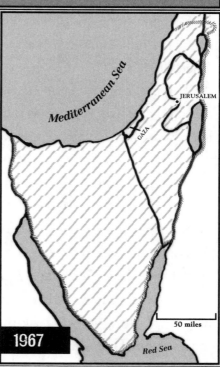

However, the Arab communities lost more in the 1948 war than they gained. Israel obtained approximately 60 percent of the territory that would have gone to the Palestinians under the UN partition. Families were displaced, their land taken. Many were sent to refugee camps in Arab countries throughout the region. Lives were disrupted forever. Palestinian statehood seemed further away.

Tensions between Israel and its Arab neighbors continued to simmer—and sometimes boil over—during the next two decades. Then, in June 1967, they erupted. Egypt, along with several other Arab states, began mobilizing their armed forces. Israel launched a preemptive strike, shattering the Egyptian air force on the ground. Known as the Six-Day War, it was over almost as soon as it began, with Israeli forces emerging victorious.

During the fighting, the decision at first was made not to try to capture the Jordanian-held Old City of Jerusalem with its religious sites. But on June 7, 1967, Israeli paratroopers entered the Old City. After brutal hand-to-hand combat, Israeli forces captured the oldest part of Jerusalem. The Temple Mount was once more in Jewish hands.

Most of the Israeli soldiers were not religious. Yet the reality that Judaism's holiest site was back in Jewish possession was overwhelming to them. There was euphoria: applause and dancing. A few soldiers flung themselves against the ancient stones and wept. As one army officer remembered after two days of fighting: "Suddenly you enter this wide open space that everyone has seen before in pictures. And though I'm not religious . . . something special had happened."

For the Arab population, it was a day of disbelief and deep despair.

And for the politicians of Israel, reality soon reared its head. Now that Israel was in command of the Old City of Jerusalem, how was it

Israeli soldiers at the Western Wall during the 1967 Six-Day War.

to be administered? And what about the expanse known as the Noble Sanctuary by some, the Temple Mount by others? What would happen to it now?

12

TURMOIL

The man who oversaw the battle for the Old City on June 7, 1967, was a veteran commander of the 1948 Arab-Israeli war named Moshe Dayan. Known for his fearlessness and his black eye patch, Dayan, though born in Israel, was not a religious Jew. When hundreds of thousands of Jews flocked to pray at the Western Wall the day it was opened for prayer—the first time in almost twenty years—Dayan was shocked. He appreciated the wall as a historical site more than as a religious one.

Of course, there were Jews who disagreed with that assessment. On June 7, the chief rabbi of the army said it was imperative to immediately blow up the mosques and shrines so the Noble Sanctuary could once again fully become the Temple Mount. Instead, Dayan insisted the Israeli flag that soldiers had stuck on the Dome of the Rock be removed, and issued a statement: "To our Arab neighbors, Israel extends the hand of peace and to all people of all faiths, we guarantee full freedom of worship. We have not come to conquer the holy places of others, but to live with others in harmony." Ten days later, he met with the leaders of the Waqf and, sitting shoeless at the

Al-Aqsa Mosque, Dayan told them that while Jerusalem would remain united under Israeli control, they would continue to have the final say over the Noble Sanctuary.

Since the early days of prayer at the Western Wall, centuries before, Jewish visitors had put slips of paper with prayers and wishes written on them into the crevices between the stones. The day the Western Wall was secured, Moshe Dayan had slipped a note between its stones. He wrote, "May peace descend on the House of Israel."

As anyone who follows current events knows, peace has not come

Israeli bulldozers clear the area in front of the Western Wall after the end of the Six-Day War.

to the Middle East. After the Six-Day War ended, a number of families living in the Arab Quarter of the Old City were moved to new homes so their houses could be demolished to create a large open space in front of the Western Wall to accommodate the throngs who wanted to come and pray. The Muslims of Jerusalem naturally felt threatened by the Israelis' push to extend their presence in what had only recently been Muslim territory. Radical political groups like the Palestine Liberation Organization began making guerrilla attacks on Israel. Jewish religious extremists felt that this was the moment to build a third temple on the Mount—after clearing it of Muslim religious sites. They were unsuccessful, but Dayan's hope for peace quickly passed.

While Israel has declared that Jerusalem is its capital, there is much worldwide disagreement with that sentiment, including at the United Nations, which considers Israel's decision about Jerusalem as the state's capital illegal. Still, there are many religionists who believe that having Jerusalem back in Jewish hands was preordained by God. Evangelical Christians consider that the Second Coming of Christ is drawing near because of this. According to this theology, once a third temple is built, there will be a huge battle in which the forces of God and good will defeat the Antichrist.

In 1969, an Evangelical Christian from Australia decided the end-time wasn't coming quickly enough and moved things forward by setting the Al-Aqsa Mosque on fire. Riots followed.

In 1972, a Palestinian group murdered eleven Israeli team members at the Munich Olympics.

In 1973, Egypt attacked Israel on Yom Kippur, the holiest day on the Jewish calendar. A war with heavy casualties on both sides ended in a cease-fire.

In 1977, with the help of United States president Jimmy Carter, Israeli premier Menachem Begin and Egyptian president Anwar Sadat began negotiating a permanent peace treaty. As always, however, there were forces who did not wish to see peace: In 1981, Sadat was assassinated by a Muslim fundamentalist. In 1982, an Israeli soldier shot two Muslim worshippers on the Noble Sanctuary, which led to rioting.

Palestinian protesters during the first intifada, 1987.

In 1987, in response to Jewish settlers building on their land, Palestinians started an uprising called an intifada. Extremists on both sides became angrier and more hardened in their positions: Israelis to secure as much land as possible with the effect of pushing Palestinians into small, crowded areas; the Palestinians and their supporters to destroy Israel.

Progress toward peace was made in the 1990s. The Oslo Accords set a path forward for resolution of ongoing issues like borders, settlements, and the government of Jerusalem. But there were many on both sides who did not want negotiation. Israeli premier Yitzhak Rabin was assassinated by an ultra-nationalist Jewish fanatic in 1995; Rabin's efforts for peace were recognized by the presence of Jordan's King Hussein and Egypt's President Hosni Mubarak at his funeral. But instead of building on the tragedy, the destruction and death have continued for more than twenty years.

Trouble has often centered on the Temple Mount/Noble Sanctuary. In the decades that followed Israel's 1967 entry into the Old City of Jerusalem, Palestinian leaders and scholars began to argue that there was never a Jewish temple there at all. In 2016, Arab countries succeeded in pushing a resolution through the UN cultural agency that cast doubt on the historical presence of a Jewish temple and on Jewish ties to the Temple Mount. The idea behind the resolution was that if there was no temple, then Israel had no claim to that sacred space.

Archaeology continues to find evidence to the contrary, but the passion surrounding the Temple Mount makes efforts to find solutions to conflict even more difficult. As one author said, "Dig a centimeter beneath the debate over antiquities, and then you hit a debate over whom the Mount belongs to, a centimeter beneath that is the war over whom the entire country belongs to."

Archaeological excavations along the Western Wall have continued to unearth amazing discoveries, including a second-century Roman street. An underground tunnel from Herod's time, running the length of the Western Wall, was opened so tourists could visit. But as the tunnel became a popular attraction, it was apparent that more safety exits were needed. The Israeli government knew that the Palestinians would consider an attempt to build a new exit (which would open into the Muslim Quarter of the city) a provocation, and at first held off. When the exit project was authorized in 1996 by another, more hard-line Israeli government, it set off riots in which eighty people were killed.

The Israeli side was distressed when the Waqf went ahead with a plan to transform Solomon's Stables into the Marwani Mosque. Then in September 2000, Israeli prime minister Ariel Sharon decided to visit the Temple Mount—with hundreds of security police. Although Israel was told by Muslim security that Sharon's visit would not be a problem as long as he didn't attempt to enter any of the buildings on the Noble Sanctuary, the Muslim population saw it differently, reacting to Sharon's statement: "It is the holiest site in Judaism and it is the right of every Jew to visit the Temple Mount." Within days a second intifada began. Thousands of Palestinians and Israelis were killed before the intifada wound to an end in 2005.

Whatever name it is known by, the Temple Mount or the Noble Sanctuary, this place of prayer and worship has too often been an expanse of destruction and death. Its history cannot be changed, but there are many people—Jews, Christians, Muslims—who believe that this is not just a site where brutal events have taken place. Instead, they think it is the spot where the world itself will begin to end.

Could they be right?

Graffiti in the Old City of Jerusalem showing the Jewish Star of David on the Dome of the Rock—a reference to the intractable and continuing conflict over the site and the ancient city that surrounds it.

13

THE WORLD TO COME

Most religious people, no matter their faith, are content to let God decide how the world will end.

But it is possible to imagine a scenario in which the most radical religious elements put into motion their feverish end-of-the-world dreams. And those dreams take them to Jerusalem, to the Temple Mount, and to the rock where it all began.

Jewish tradition says that in the last days, the Messiah, an anointed one sent from God, will come to Jerusalem to usher in an age of peace and harmony for all humankind. In Christianity, Jesus is recognized as that Messiah, and his followers believe that he will return to earth, bringing with him the Kingdom of God. In Islam, an angel will blow his trumpet from the rock under the Dome. That will signal a day of resurrection, and Allah's judgment on all of humanity.

For some people, it is not too long a step from waiting for the world to come, to thinking that it is their duty to hurry things along. The movement to rebuild the Jewish temple on the Temple Mount is still relatively small, but it is gaining strength. Of course, building a new temple would mean destroying or moving the Dome of the Rock and the Al-Aqsa Mosque. We have seen the anger and fighting engendered by the excavation of a tunnel or a walk on the Temple Mount by an Israeli prime minister. Any destructive move toward Islamic sites (some have already been planned but were foiled) could lead to catastrophe.

Some Christians believe the Temple Mount is the exact spot where Jesus will return. They point to the biblical verse Isaiah 2:2, which says, "In the last days, the mountain of the house of the Lord will be established as the chief of the mountains . . . And all the nations will stream to it." Removing Islamic shrines might be a priority for those who want to hasten the Second Coming of Jesus.

Muslims also have beliefs surrounding the end-time, centered in Jerusalem, and see it as their right and duty to protect their holy sites at their Noble Sanctuary. At the present time, it is possible but difficult for non-Muslims to visit the Noble Sanctuary. Only Muslims are allowed inside the Dome of the Rock, so the rock itself is available to be seen by observers of only one of the three religions that honor its history.

The Temple Mount has been called "potentially the most volatile 35 acres on earth." One noted archaeological scholar added that if the word *potentially* was deleted, the statement would be even more accurate. If a local war breaks out over these religious sites, it could quickly ignite a larger war that would draw in countries from around the world.

Judaism, Christianity, and Islam all see themselves as being the descendants of one man who made a covenant with God: Abraham. Yet instead of honoring a common heritage, these groups have allowed disputes and differences to take center stage. Is there any hope for peace in this holiest and bloodiest of places?

One path might be to make Jerusalem an international city, something the original UN declaration in 1947 called for. However, as it has since 1980, Israel maintains that "a complete and united Jerusalem" should be the capital of Israel. The Palestinians see Jerusalem as the capital of their future state. The United Nations recommends that a multinational organization, under UN auspices, govern the city. Free and open access to the religious sites of the Jews, Christians, and Muslims would be a part of the plan. Although this idea has been discussed in the erratic peace talks between the Israelis and the Palestinians over the decades, neither side has been willing to relinquish what control it has.

Another proposal has been that the Israelis and Palestinians jointly govern Jerusalem, though how exactly this would work has not been established. This, too, seems like an idea almost impossible to implement, considering the hostility and distrust on both sides.

Yet if peace could come to the Temple Mount, the Noble Sanctuary, what a gift to the world that would be. Is there a place to start? Is there any common ground to build upon?

Well, there is one thing. Judaism, Christianity, and Islam all take as one of their highest principles some variation on the Golden Rule: do unto others as you would have them do unto you.

The Jews sometimes put it as: "Do nothing to other people that you would not like having done to you."

In the Christian Bible, Jesus tells his followers: "Love your neighbor as you love yourself."

Muhammad said to his followers in his farewell speech: "Hurt no one so that no one will hurt you."

The Golden Rule is simple, but it is not always easy to follow. On the Temple Mount, the Noble Sanctuary, Jews, Christians, and

Muslims have often turned the Golden Rule inside out, fostering hate instead of love and hurting those whose beliefs differ from their own. If a day comes when the children of Abraham can treat one another with compassion and see one another as individuals—men, women, and children whose dreams, fears, and longings are like their own—then perhaps that elusive peace will be possible.

TIME LINE

c. 1010–c. 970 BCE Reign of King David

c. 1000 BCE David conquers Jerusalem and unites Israel and Judah

c. 970–c. 930 BCE Reign of King Solomon

c. 966–c. 959 BCE Construction of First Temple under Solomon

772 BCE Assyrian invasion of Israel

597 BCE Babylonian invasion of Judaea

586 BCE Destruction of First Temple by the Babylonians

538–515 BCE Construction of Second Temple

332 BCE Conquest of Jerusalem by Greeks under Alexander the Great

323 BCE Death of Alexander the Great and beginning of rule of Judaea by Ptolemaic and Seleucid kings

164 BCE Maccabees revolt and take control of Judaea from the Seleucids

63 BCE Judaea becomes part of the Roman Empire

39–4 BCE Reign of Herod the Great

20 BCE–64 CE Reconstruction of the Temple Mount and renovation of Second Temple under Herod's orders

c. 4 BCE–c. 30 CE Life of Jesus of Nazareth

66–73 CE Jewish rebellion against Rome, ending at the Siege of Masada

70 Destruction of Second Temple by the Romans under Titus

130 Rebuilding of Jerusalem as Aelia Capitolina begins under Roman emperor Hadrian

313 Roman emperor Constantine issues edict allowing Christians and others the freedom to follow their religious beliefs

326 Restoration of Christian sites in Jerusalem by Roman empress Helena

c. 570–632 Life of Muhammad

638 Conquest of Jerusalem by Muslims under Caliph Umar I and construction of the first mosque on the Noble Sanctuary

688–692 Construction of the Dome of the Rock

1096–1099 First Crusade

1099 Siege and destruction of Jerusalem by Christian crusaders

1187 Reoccupation of Jerusalem by Muslims under Saladin

1517 Jerusalem becomes part of Ottoman Empire

1535 Rebuilding of Jerusalem under Suleiman begins

1914–1918 First World War; Jerusalem comes under British control

1917 Balfour Declaration favoring the establishment of a Jewish homeland in Palestine

1939–1945 Second World War

1947 Partition of Palestine into Jewish and Arab states, followed by civil war

1948 Israel declares itself a state

1948–1949 War between Israel and Arab nations; Jordan takes control of Old City of Jerusalem

1967 Six-Day War between Israel and Arab nations; Israel takes control of Old City of Jerusalem

NOTES

Chapter 1: Before the Temple

5   *There are places on earth*: The discussion of sacred spaces is informed by the discussion in Armstrong, *Jerusalem*, 7–8.

6   *He was to take his son*: The story of the binding of Isaac is told in Genesis 22. It is also mentioned in the New Testament's Epistle to the Hebrews 11:17. The Islamic version differs from the biblical story: Abraham tells his son about God's command and the son agrees to be sacrificed. This submission is commemorated on the Islamic calendar during Eid al-Adha. In Islamic tradition, the son to be sacrificed is the firstborn, identified as Ishmael.

7   *Jacob laid his head down*: The story of Jacob's dream is told in Genesis 28:10–22. Jacob is also considered a patriarch in the New Testament and in the Islamic holy book, the Quran.

7   *But one thing this settlement*: The PBS television documentary *Jerusalem: Center of the World* provides a visual introduction to the Gihon Spring.

8   *Pieces of clay cuneiform*: The cuneiform tablets are discussed in Armstrong, *Jerusalem*, 14.

9   *But one baby was saved*: The story of Moses is told in the Book of Exodus. Moses's story is also recounted later in the Quran, where he is considered a prophet.

10   *According to the Bible story*: God's description of the ark is given in Exodus 25:10–22.

11   *"the ark of Your strength"*: Psalms 132:8. International Standard Version Bible.

11   *an inscribed stone*: The story of the stele from the Tel Dan in northern Israel is told in Shanks, *Jerusalem's Temple Mount*, 154.

11   *There are many heroes*: David's story is told in the biblical books of 1 and 2 Samuel; 1 Kings; and 1 Chronicles.

11   *David first appears*: David's encounter with Goliath is told in 1 Samuel 17.

13   *"Even the blind and the lame"*: 2 Samuel 5:6. International Standard Version Bible.

13   *"Here I am"*: 2 Samuel 7:2. New International Bible.

Chapter 2: Solomon's Temple

17   *The king, who perhaps*: The story of David buying the temple site from the Jebusite king is told in 1 Chronicles 21–25.

17   *Then, according to*: A description of David's extensive plans for the temple is given in 1 Chronicles 28.

18   *The most famous was*: The story of King Solomon and the dispute over the baby is told in 1 Kings 3:16–28. Solomon's wives are mentioned in 1 Kings 11:3.

18   *Though Solomon's time*: King Solomon appears in many other media, including the oft-told *Arabian Nights* stories; H. Rider Haggard's novel *King Solomon's Mines* (1885; Penguin Classics 2008); Rudyard Kipling's *Just So Stories*; the movie *Solomon and Sheba* (1959); George Frideric Handel's 1748 oratorio *Solomon*; and the Japanese manga series *Magi: The Labyrinth of Magic*.

18   *It was a magnificent*: Descriptions of the temple appear in 1 Kings 6–7 and 2 Chronicles 2–4. All the books in the bibliography (pages 128–29) pertaining to the Temple Mount offer discussion and interpretation of the temple, including its reported decorations, symbolism, and uses.

24   *In sections of the*: Mentions of the temple appear in 2 Kings 11:1–4, 10–11; 18:16. Most scholars agree that Kings is more historically accurate than earlier sections of the Hebrew Bible.

24   *A private antiquities*: A full discussion of the Jehoash Stone appears in Shanks, *Jerusalem's Temple Mount*, 143–50. It gives great insight into the contentious arguments surrounding contemporary archaeological finds.

25   *"I have indeed built"*: Solomon's dedication speech, or prayer, is found in 1 Kings 8:13. English Standard Bible.

Chapter 3: The Fall—and Rise—of the Temple

30   *"The stones of the sanctuary"*: Lamentations 4:1. King James Bible.

30   *One contemporary theory*: The fascinating story of the ark and its possible location in Zimbabwe is told by professor of Oriental and African studies Tudor Parfitt, *The Lost Ark of the Covenant*.

31   *"By the rivers of Babylon"*: Psalms 137:1. King James Bible.

32   *"Who is left among you"*: Haggai 2:3. English Standard Version Bible.

32   *The Ptolemies, though Greek*: The account of the Ptolemy king is in

3 Maccabees 3–4. The history of the Maccabees is contained in the four books of the Maccabees, which are Jewish writings, but not part of the Hebrew Bible. The story of Hanukkah appears in the first two books of the Maccabees.

33   *But in 176 BCE:* The account of the Seleucid plunder of the temple is in Grabar and Kedar, eds., *Where Heaven and Earth Meet,* 44.

Chapter 4: Herod's Temple

A word about Flavius Josephus. Much of what historians know about first-century Jewish-Roman history comes from the writings of Josephus. Born to a high-ranking Jewish family in Jerusalem, he led Jewish forces against Rome but surrendered in 67 CE. He was taken prisoner by the soon-to-be emperor of Rome, Vespasian; by 69, he was freed, and turned his loyalty to Rome, though in his writings he shows a Jewish viewpoint. As an eyewitness to many events, including the destruction of Jerusalem, he had a unique perspective from which to write. That said, many modern historians believe Josephus had a tendency to exaggeration, especially when it came to numbers—for example, the number of people who died in catastrophic events.

40   *The temple was the focus:* Jewish citizens' concerns about the rebuilding of the temple appear in Josephus, *Antiquities of the Jews,* 11:1.

40   *As the ancient historian Josephus:* Descriptions of Herod's preparations for the temple are given in Josephus, *Antiquities of the Jews,* 15:11–2.

40   *The first thing Herod's architects:* Ritmeyer, "Quarrying and Transporting Stones for Herod's Temple Mount."

44   *Archaeologists have found signs:* The warning inscription was found near the Temple Mount site in 1871; the piece is at the Istanbul Archaeology Museums in Istanbul, Turkey. Another warning notice was excavated in Jerusalem in 1935 and is on display in the Israel Museum. The Trumpeting Place inscription found in 1968 near the southern wall of the Temple Mount is believed to have been a signpost to the place for those who blew the trumpet that signified the beginning and the end of the Sabbath day. Remnants of Robinson's Arch, a stone expanse that was built along the retaining walls and led to the Royal Stoa, and stones, distinctive in their carving, are among the other discoveries from Herod's Temple.

48   *"at the first rising of the sun":* Josephus, *War of the Jews,* 5:222.

Chapter 5: Jesus at the Temple

50   *Jesus's first trip to the temple:* The story is told in Luke 2:22–39.

50   *Realizing that their son:* The story of Jesus as a boy talking to the rabbis at the temple is told in Luke 2:41–52.

51   *Only days before:* Much of what is known about Herod comes from the works of the historian Josephus.

54   *This dramatic display:* The story of Jesus's encounter with the Sanhedrin is told in Matthew 26:57 as well as in the other three gospels.

Chapter 6: Destruction

56   *"Do you see all these great buildings?"*: Mark 13:2. New International Bible.

59   *"Through the roar of the flames"*: Cornfeld, ed., *Josephus, the Jewish War*.

Chapter 7: Forgotten

64   *"These Jews would tear"*: From a document found in the Cairo Genhiza, a repository for religious documents. Armstrong, *Jerusalem*, 170.

65   *In 312, according:* Although there are several versions of this story, historical consensus is that Constantine had a dream or vision in which he saw a cross of light and the Greek words "In this sign, you shall conquer." The sign was a monogram of the Greek letters *chi* (X) and *rho* (P), the first two letters of the Greek word for Christ, which were used as Christian symbols.

Chapter 8: The Noble Sanctuary

71   *A merchant by trade:* A vivid description of Muhammad in the Hira cave is given in Aslan, *No god but God*, 34.

71   *Allah, the Arabic name:* The word *Allah* is thought to be derived by contraction from *al ilāh*, which means "the God."

71   *"An invisible presence"*: Aslan, *No god but God*, 34.

73   *This particular story:* "The Night Journey" is retold in many sources, including the one I've referenced, Lundquist, *The Temple of Jerusalem*, 185–87.

77   *This peaceful entry:* Umar's visit to the Temple Mount. Ibid., 188, and Armstrong, *Jerusalem*, 229.

78   *"a four-sided house"*: From "The Pilgrimage of Arculfus," in Armstrong, *Jerusalem*, 231.

78   *"wanted monuments that were unique"*: Ibid., 237.

80   "the most beautiful and perfect achievement": Shanks, Jerusalem's Temple Mount, 9.

81   "Its exterior, which reaches": Armstrong, Jerusalem, 241.

Chapter 9: The Temple Mount Retaken

82   "God wills it!": Montefiore, Jerusalem, 219.

85   After a few weeks: A vivid (and disturbing) account of the Crusaders' siege of Jerusalem appears in Montefiore, Jerusalem, 221–25.

87   all sorts of legends: The Knights Templar have appeared in books, including Dan Brown's The Da Vinci Code; the video game series Assassin's Creed; and the movies Indiana Jones and the Last Crusade and National Treasure.

Chapter 10: Saladin and Suleiman

91   "We shall deal with you": "The Crusades through Arab Eyes," tr. by Jon Rothschild, in Armstrong, Jerusalem, 293.

Chapter 11: Two Peoples, Two Homelands

99   In 1840: Population figures, Armstrong, Jerusalem, 352.

103   In 1917, after the British: The Balfour Declaration, newworldencyclopedia .org/entry/Balfour_Declaration.

109   "Suddenly you enter": Montefiore, Jerusalem, 518.

Chapter 12: Turmoil

110   "To our Arab neighbors": sixdaywar.org/content/ReunificationJerusalem.asp.

111   "May peace descend": Montefiore, Jerusalem, 513.

114   In the decades that followed: Discussion of whether the temple really existed in Shanks, Jerusalem's Temple Mount, 4.

114   "Dig a centimeter": Ibid., 5.

115   "It is the holiest site": theguardian.com/world/2000/sep/29/israel.

Chapter 13: The World to Come

118   "In the last days": Isaiah 2:2. New American Standard Bible.

118   The Temple Mount has been called: Ostling, "Time for a New Temple."

118   One noted archaeological: Shanks, Jerusalem's Temple Mount, 5.

BIBLIOGRAPHY

Books

* Asterisk indicates books for young readers.

Armstrong, Karen. *Jerusalem: One City, Three Faiths*. New York: Ballantine Books, 1997.

Aslan, Reza. *No god but God: The Origins, Evolution, and Future of Islam*. New York: Random House, 2005.

Bahat, Dan, and Shalom Sabar. *Jerusalem Stone and Spirit: 3000 Years of History and Art*. New York: Rizzoli, 1997.

Carroll, James. *Jerusalem, Jerusalem: How the Ancient City Ignited Our Modern World*. Boston: Houghton Mifflin, 2011.

* Cooper, Ilene. *The Dead Sea Scrolls*. New York: Morrow Junior Books, 1997.

Cornfeld, Gaalya, ed. *Josephus, the Jewish War*. Grand Rapids, MI: Zondervan, 1982.

* Dué, Andrea. *The Atlas of the Bible Lands: History, Daily Life and Traditions*. New York: Peter Bedrick Books, 1999.

Goldhill, Simon. *The Temple of Jerusalem*. Cambridge, MA: Harvard University Press, 2004.

Grabar, Oleg, and Benjamin Z. Kedar, eds. *Where Heaven and Earth Meet: Jerusalem's Sacred Esplanade*. Austin: University of Texas Press, 2009.

* Green, Robert. *Herod the Great*. New York: Franklin Watts, 1996.

Hamblin, William J., and David Rolph Seely. *Solomon's Temple: Myth and History*. London: Thames & Hudson, 2007.

Lundquist, John M. *The Temple of Jerusalem: Past, Present, and Future*. Santa Barbara, CA: Praeger, 2008.

Montefiore, Simon Sebag. *Jerusalem: The Biography*. New York: Knopf, 2011.

Parfitt, Tudor. *The Lost Ark of the Covenant: Solving the 2,500-Year-Old Mystery of the Fabled Biblical Ark*. New York: HarperCollins, 2009.

Shanks, Hershel. *Jerusalem: An Archaeological Biography*. New York: Random House, 1995.

Shanks, Hershel. *Jerusalem's Temple Mount: From Solomon to the Golden Dome*. New York: Continuum, 2007.

* Slavik, Diane. *Daily Life in Ancient and Modern Jerusalem*. Minneapolis: Runestone Press/Lerner, 2001.

Walker, Peter. *The Story of the Holy Land: A Visual History*. Oxford: Lion Hudson, 2013.

* Wolf, Bernard. *If I Forget Thee, O Jerusalem*. New York: Dutton, 1998.

Articles

"The Holy Land: Crossroads of Faith and Conflict." *National Geographic*, 2009.

Ostling, Richard N. "Time for a New Temple." *Time*, Oct. 16, 1989. content .time.com/time/magazine/article/0,9171,958787,00.html.

Ritmeyer, Leen. "Quarrying and Transporting Stones for Herod's Temple Mount." *Biblical Archaeology Review*, November/December 1989. biblicalarchaeology.org/daily/biblical-sites-places/temple-at-jerusalem /the-stones-of-herod%E2%80%99s-temple-reveal-temple-mount-history/.

Audiovisual Materials

Jerusalem: Center of the World. PBS, 2011. pbs.org/show/jerusalem-center-of-the -world/.

Websites

Biblical Archaeology Society: biblicalarchaeology.org

CAMERA (Committee for Accuracy in Middle East Reporting in America): sixdaywar.org/content/ReunificationJerusalem.asp

The Guardian: theguardian.com/world/2000/sep/29/israel

Jewish Virtual Library: jewishvirtuallibrary.org/jsource/Society_&_Culture/geo /Mount.html

New World Encyclopedia: newworldencyclopedia.org

The New York Times: nytimes.com

The Noble Sanctuary: noblesanctuary.com

The Smithsonian: smithsonianmag.com/history/what-is-beneath-the-temple -mount-920764/?no-ist

INDEX